Monographic Journals of the Near East   *Occasional Papers* 1/2 (November 1981)

MAKING STONE VASES: ETHNOARCHAEOLOGICAL STUDIES
AT AN ALABASTER WORKSHOP IN UPPER EGYPT

by

Thomas R. Hester

and

Robert F. Heizer

This monograph, based on field work in Egypt in 1972, provides a description of alabaster vase-making at a contemporary workshop in the village of Sheik Abd el Gurna, western Thebes. The study documents the technology employed in this local folk craft and relates the techniques to stone vase-making in ancient Egypt.

TABLE OF CONTENTS

PREFACE*

The past decade has seen a renewed interest in research involving the study of ancient technologies. One avenue of inquiry which has produced important new data in this field has been ethnoarchaeology. The study published here began as an effort to document an interesting folk industry, but as we worked we became intrigued by the potential for applying these data to "ethnotechnological" research. Thus, while we did the 1972 field work with no preconceived ethnoarchaeological research design, we trust that the resulting monograph will have some utility in this field. We hope that further work can be done.

After our manuscript was completed, we learned of the following publication: *Egyptian Stone Vessels, Predynastic Period to Dynasty III* (by Ali Bdel-Rahman Hassanian El-Khauli), Verlag Philip von Zabern, Mainz/Rheim, 1978 (Vols. I-III). We have not had the opportunity to examine these volumes. However, our colleague, Dr. Salvatori describes the volumes as primarily a catalog of Egyptian stone vessels, accompanied by numerous drawings and photographs. In Vol. II, there is a brief section (pp. 789-801) entitled, "Manufacture of Stone Vessels—Ancient and Modern." We have reprinted this as an appendix to the present study.

Thomas R. Hester
Robert F. Heizer
May, 1979

I. INTRODUCTION

In 1971, during the course of a research project involving the Colossi of Memnon (Heizer *et al.* 1973; Heizer, Stross and Hester 1973), we visited a small workshop area in the village of Sheik Abd el Gurna on the western plain of Thebes in upper Egypt.[1] At this workshop, vessels and other objects of alabaster were being made by hand. We took a number of photographs and recorded some initial observations regarding the workshop activities. We were struck by the fact that the craftsmen were producing these stone artifacts by hand, utilizing techniques which seemed to us little different than those we had seen depicted in reliefs on the walls of Old Kingdom tombs.

Thus, in February, 1972, when we returned to Egypt to continue our study of the Colossi of Memnon, we decided to make a detailed record of the alabaster workshops at Sheik Abd el Gurna (Fig. 1). Prof. John A. Graham (University of California, Berkeley) aided us in this effort. The research at the workshops had two major goals: (1) a thorough photographic documentation accomplished by taking several hundred black and white photographs and

---

*This monograph is dedicated to Dr. Robert F. Heizer, Professor Emeritus, University of California, Berkeley, who died on July 18, 1979, only a short while after completion of the full draft of the manuscript on which this monograph is based.—Thomas R. Hester, San Antonio, Texas, May, 1980.

[1] The Colossi of Memnon research was supported in 1971-1972 by grants from the National Geographic Society, Washington, D.C.

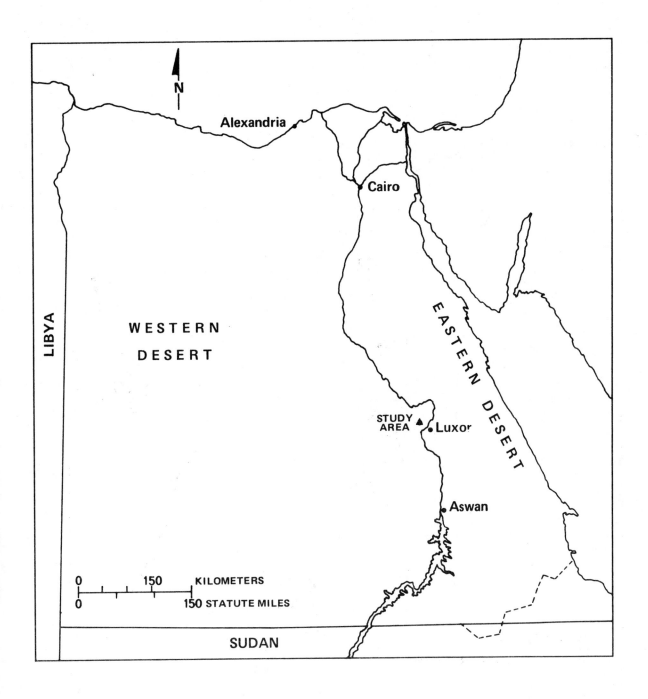

Figure 1.   Map of Egypt, with the Study Area Indicated.

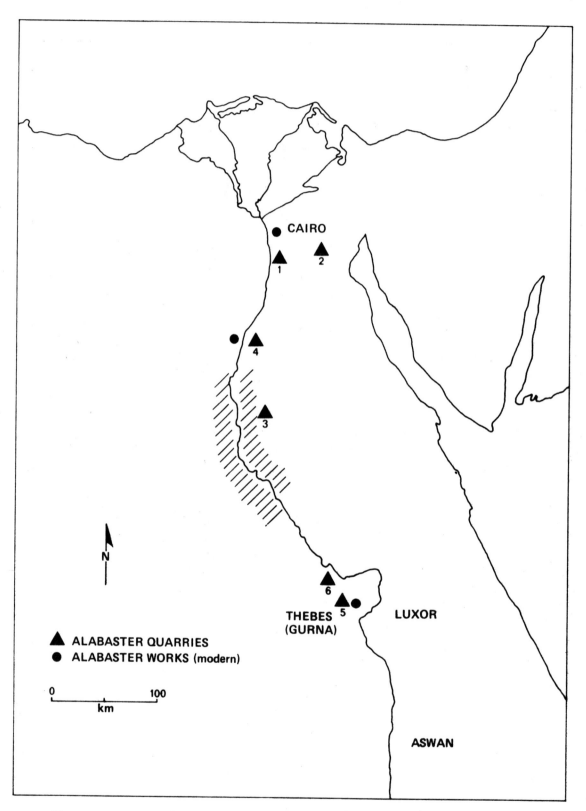

Figure 2. Locations of Ancient Alabaster Quarries and Modern Alabaster Works in Egypt.
1. Helwan; 2. Cairo-Suez desert; 3. Hatnub vicinity (many quarries, apparently on both sides of the river); 4. east of Maghagha (at Wadi Moathil); 5. three miles from Wadiyien, opposite Luxor; 6. mountains of Nag' Hammadi.

color slides, and by making a record of the alabaster-working on 16 mm film;[2] (2) a careful written account, through direct observation and informant interviews, of the techniques and sequence of alabaster vessel manufacture and an overall study of the alabaster industry.

We felt that this research would benefit the study of alabaster technology in ancient Egypt. Such studies of material culture, in primitive and nonindustrial societies, designed to aid in archaeological interpretation have been done in various parts of the world for many years. More recently, this field of investigation has intensified and broadened (including research in modern, industrialized societies) and has become known as ethnoarchaeology (see Hester, Heizer and Graham 1975:10); a sample of some important studies include the publications of Donnan and Clewlow (1974), Yellen (1977) and Gould (1978).

II. ANCIENT EGYPTIAN USE OF ALABASTER

Alabaster was extensively utilized by the ancient Egyptian populations. As a construction material it was used for lining passages and rooms, this beginning in the early dynastic period and lasting well into New Kingdom times (Lucas and Harris 1962:59). Large sculptures were sometimes made of alabaster. An example is the 60-ton alabaster statue of Djehutihetep, depicted in a 12th century tomb painting at El Bersheh (see Heizer 1966:Fig. 10). Another major use was in the manufacture of vessels destined to be placed as funerary offerings in elite tombs and, according to Harris (1961:77), "alabaster was the classic material for unguent vessels." According to Montet (1925:147) the manufacture of stone vases had been perfected to a high degree in the first dynasty and still fluorished in the Ramesside period. Even later manufacture of alabaster vases, canopic jars and the like are evidenced in the displays at the Louvre of such specimens from the Säitic dynasties, as late as the fourth century B.C.

An example of just how extensively the alabaster resource was used comes from the Old Kingdom, particularly in tombs at the site of Saqqara. In one of the galleries of the third dynasty Step Pyramid of Zoser at the site, about 30,000 alabaster vessels (roughly 90 tons) were found (Firth, Quibell and Lauer 1935:130; Quibell 1935:76-77).

III. GEOLOGIC SOURCES OF ALABASTER

Egyptian alabaster is, in geologic terms, a calcite. According to Lucas and Harris (1962:59), it is a "compact crystalline form of calcium carbonate, white or yellowish white in colour, translucent in thin sections and frequently banded." The same authors (ibid.:59-60) have described in some detail the various geologic sources of alabaster exploited by ancient and modern-day Egyptians. They note its occurrence in the Sinai and at a series of localities on the east and west sides of the Nile. The approximate locations of these sources (and ancient quarries) are shown in Fig. 2. They include a locality in the Cairo-Suez desert (also apparently used in modern times); a source near Wadi Moathil (a branch of the Wadi Sennur), due east of Maghagha; an area of ca. 90 miles from Minia to south of Asiut in which there are signs of

---

[2] Our film-making efforts met only moderate success. The rented camera turned out to be faulty and only about one-half of the exposed footage turned out to be of any value. This still awaits editing.

many quarries, with the most important being at Hatnub (15 miles east of El Amarna; the Hatnub source was the principal one up to the time of the New Kingdom, according to Harris 1961:78) and at Guata near Wadi Asiut; a source in the mountains near Nag' Hammadi; and a quarry used in modern times three miles behind Wadiyein (a branch of Wadi el Muluk, on the west side of the Nile opposite Luxor). There is also an important ancient alabaster quarry at Wadi Gerrawi near Helwan. This quarry has been described in detail by Erman (1894:470):

"A little southward of Turah nearly opposite Dahshur, surrounded by steep limestone cliffs, the Wadi Gerraui stretches into the mountains. In this valley the old alabaster quarries were discovered in modern days by Schweinfurth; they lie three or four hours' journey from the Nile valley, with which they were connected by a road which can still be traced in places. About an hour's journey below the quarries proper are the ruins of the stone huts of the workmen. A very strong wall, formed of blocks of stone piled up, and covered on the outside with squared stone, forms a dam across the valley at this point, and presumably served to intercept the stream formed by the winter rain, and thus to store the water for both workmen and draught cattle. The greatness of this work— the dam is about 30 feet high, 216 feet broad, and nearly 140 feet thick—shows that at one time great importance was attached to the quarries of the Wadi Gerraui. This may have been during a period when the finer alabaster afterwards obtained from the town of Hat-nub, the *gold house*, was as yet unknown. Even the latter quarries were undoubtedly exhausted under King Pepy of the 6th dynasty."

Undoubtedly, some of the alabaster used in contemporary alabaster workshops is derived from quarries opened in ancient times. Others, like the one at Wadiyein near Luxor, have been utilized only in modern times; Lucas and Harris (1962:60) provide a description of this locality:

"A white translucent alabaster occurs in small amounts and is worked on a small scale for vases (often sold as ancient ones) about three miles behind Wadiyein which branches off Wadi el Muluk, on the west side of the Nile opposite Luxor. There is no evidence of ancient working."

This modern source may supply some of the alabaster to the contemporary workshops; however, it does not appear to have been the source, at least in recent years, for the alabaster used in the workshops we studied.

IV. ALABASTER-WORKING IN ANCIENT EGYPT

The widespread use of alabaster, and the sometimes massive numbers of objects required to be made from it, meant that a craft specialization centering on alabaster-working did develop. Unfortunately, we do not have any very good accounts of the excavation of ancient alabaster workshops at Egyptian sites. There are some brief mentions of excavated areas which probably functioned as such, e.g., at Meydum (Petrie, MacKay and Wainwright 1910:44) and Hierakonpolis (Quibell and Green 1902:17-18). The Hierakonpolis occurrence is described as follows:

Room 12 of group 89 is a vase-grinder's workshop. The room itself is 2.6 x 2.1 meters (102 x 82 inches, 5 x 4 cubits). Access was gained to it by a passage with a door at the southern angle of the room. The sandstone socket of this door was found in place. . . .

Round the room ran a bench of beaten earth 0.8 m (2-1/2 feet) above the floor. This bench projects considerably in the W. angle and to a lesser degree in the S. angle. The upper parts of these projections have cup-like hollows in which were vase borers, such as shown in Pl. LXII. That marked I. was of chert. It stood with working surface upwards in the depression in the bench; under it was a quantity of sand that had been used as the abrading material. On the top of the borer were two rough pieces of chert. Near to it (marked 2) was an oblong corn grinder. The borer marked 3 on the drawing was of diorite. Both sides had been used as working surfaces. Little or no sand was found in the socket or depression in the bench.

From the fact of the bench being 0.8 above the floor, it seems as if the workmen must have stood to their task; the squatting position is, however, that represented on the reliefs, when the operation of vase making is represented.

In the earth, from the level of the foot of the walls, up to and on the present ground surface, numerous fragments of hard stone vases and bowls were found. Similar fragments, as well as the vase borers scattered all over the site, afford evidence of the extent of this vase-making industry." (*ibid.*).

In a more recent review of the Hierakonpolis data, Adams (1974a, 1974b) has provided some additional detail on the "vase-grinder's workshop" described by Quibell and Green. For example, in her publication of Green's field notes (Adams 1974b), the "grinder's workshop" is described as being a "small room . . . 6 x 2.1" (meters) in plan, rather than the 2.6 x 2.1 dimensions given above. Green's notes (*ibid.*:66) suggests that the "quantity of sand" (see above) found associated with one of the borers resulted from "sandstone socket so much disintegrated by wear as to become mere wet sand on water, appears to be origin of sand under grinder." Green's notes include a rough plan and diagrammatic side view sketches of this apparent workshop, and he notes the occurrence of other artifacts, including pottery fragments and flint specimens. Unfortunately, Green's notes shed little additional light on the workshop, and it seems that Quibell did not even keep field notes, or at least their whereabouts remain unknown (Adams 1974b:1).

There may have been other workshops in the "town" at Hierakonpolis, as Green recorded (Adams 1974b:77) "two pot borers" in another structure. Associated with these were a fine diorite "pounding stone," "another pounding stone of rough flint," and a "flat corn rubber." These were among a group of potter vessels in an alcove. One can only speculate as to whether the "pounding stones" and "corn rubber" were actually tools related to the alabaster vase-making process. Desmond Clark (personal communication) has suggested that the "pounders" and "corn rubber" might be old, worn-out objects which were put to some sort of secondary use in the workshop. Elsewhere in the town, Green's notes recorded the presence in the "S. room" of another structure of "numerous pot grinders" (*ibid.*:76).

Although we have inadequate archaeological data on alabaster (and other stone) workshops, a rich record of the manufacture of stone vessels is preserved in bas relief sculptures on the walls of Old Kingdom tombs (cf. Davies 1902:Pl.14; Blackman 1914:Pl.5; Klebs 1915:Abb.66; Blackman and Apted 1953:Pl.XVII).

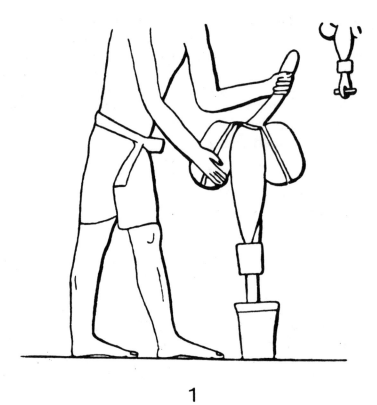

1

2

Figure 3.   Stone Vase Manufacture in Ancient Egypt.
1. adapted from Childe (1954); 2. redrawn from Davies (1902); this scene is found in the Tomb of Aba, north wall, east side.

We have reproduced several of these scenes in Figs. 3-5. Analysis of such scenes, along with the study of excavated vase borer bits and alabaster artifacts, have permitted several archaeologists to comment on the stone vase-working process. Since our knowledge of ancient Egyptian vase-manufacturing technology is still so limited (cf. Harding 1971:242) and has not been thoroughly summarized elsewhere, we have chosen to assemble a selection of previously published interpretations.

Davis (1902:18-19) has interpreted the vase-making process as depicted in the tomb of Aba at Deir el Gebrâwi (see Fig. 3,1):

> "The process of grinding out the interior of large stone vases by means of a kind of centre-bit, is shown first in place as it was earliest among Egyptian achievements. The extraordinary mastery of this art which the prehistoric Egyptians possessed seems reflected in the employment of the picture of this drill as word-sign for "craftsman," stone-working being then confessedly the craft *par excellence*. The tool consisted of an upright rod, weighted near the top with two stones, which were loosely lashed to the stem, and so gave great momentum to the tool when rapidly revolved. The boring was done by a blade with cutting edges at both ends, which was set horizontally across the bottom of the rod, the diameter of the cylinder removed by it varying with the length of the blade employed. The stem, being steadied in the middle by one hand, was revolved by a curved crank at the top, or, in later times, by the improved method adopted in our own centre-bits. One workman here is actually using the tool; two others are exhibiting specimens of their handiwork, further examples of which are shown near them . . . From the colour and markings the material seems to be alabaster, which is otherwise improbable."

From a paper on rotary motion published by Childe (1954:192) in volume 1 of *A History of Technology*, we have extracted the following comments:

> "From Egypt in particular, the stone vase-making processes are well documented by vessels in all stages of manufacture, by a variety of bits, and best of all by lively pictures from Old Kingdom and later tombs. . . . The actual grinding was still done by an abrasive—sand or sometimes emery (corundum, aluminum oxide). The bits were of flint fixed into cleft sticks. For hollowing out globular vessels, a series of graded flint crescents were employed successively as the operation proceeded. The tomb pictures show that the requisite pressure was obtained by tying a pair of heavy stones to the spindle. The hieroglyphic symbol is a picture of this device with its weights and crescent bit fixed in the forked stick . . . The craftsman's left hand grasps the top of the stick while the right hand turns it, apparently by pushing on the weights.

> In the early pictures the upper end of the stick seems curved, and this has suggested that it was used as a sort of crank handle. The swing of the arms to and fro would then be converted into rotary motion. If this interpretation is correct, the ancient Egyptians were applying true rotary motion to one sort of drilling before 2500 B.C."

J. E. Quibell (1935:77) summarizes his view of the vase-making process with the following brief remarks:

> "The outside of the vase was finished before the hollowing out of the block was commenced. On the shoulder of two vases we have noticed two horizontal grooves, opposite to one another, which as Mr. Lacau observed, were probably intended to give a good hold to the tool by which

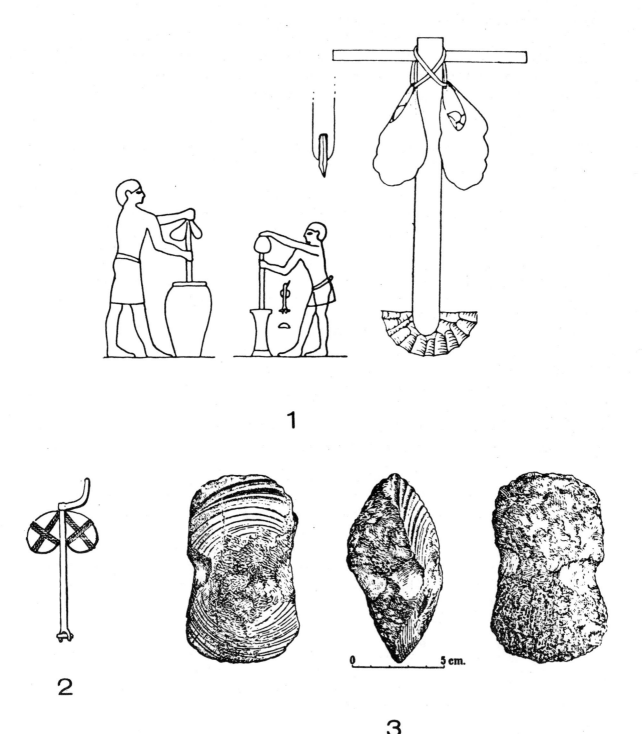

Figure 4.   Stone Vase Manufacture in Ancient Egypt.

1. adapted from Hodges (1970: Figs. 100-101); the idea of a crescentic flint bit, as shown here, is erroneous; 2. the hieroglyphic sign for ancient stone vase workers; 3. three examples of sandstone vase "borers" or bits; from Borchardt (1907: Abb. 123-124).

the block was rotated. An amethyst vase spoilt in the making . . . was finished externally, but the inside, only begun, showed a rough surface obtained by careful picking, with a point grain by grain. . . . It seems that for dressing the outer surface the vase itself was rotated, for hollowing the inside the vase was fixed, embedded in pitch or clay."

Emery, in his *Archaic Egypt* (1961:175), provides this brief summary:

"From unfinished vessels we have ascertained that the vessel was finished externally before the hollowing of the interior was begun. We know also that the rough cutting of the interior was done with the aid of a drill with a curious eccentric handle, to which two oval stones were slung with ropes. These stone weights, which splayed outwards when the drill was turned, thus provided extra motive power. The cutting head of these drills was a flint blade shaped rather like a blunt arrow-head. Such drill-heads, and stone weights, have been found in considerable quantity, and we also have pictures of the pyramid age which show the drill being worked. A tubular drill was also used for work on smaller vessels. But this method of drilling, while adequate for cutting the interior of cylindrical vases . . . would not be practical for hollowing out the inside of the larger jars. . . . How, for example, was the upward pressure obtained to cut away the interior side of the shoulders? All these problems as yet remain unanswered and are likely to remain so until perhaps the discovery of a stone vase maker's workshop which will reveal some of his methods."

Petrie (1937:2-3) offers this more extensive description:

"The mode of manufacture was usually by grinding. The form was first chipped roughly, and the surface then worked down by emery blocks. The direction of grinding was not circular, but diagonal, on prehistoric vases. On the dynastic bowls, the grinding was done circularly in a block. For hollowing the interior, many methods were followed, according to the form. The main resource was to drill out a large core from the axis, to begin with; this removed the portion which would grind away most slowly, and left a hollow into which the sludge of grinding would fall. The main part was then ground out with a block, fed with sand or emery.

In the earlier part of the 1st dynasty, the circular groove of the tube drill was carefully ground away in hollowing the interior. By the middle of the dynasty it was often left, showing as a ring in the smooth hollow. Later still, this ring mark was regarded as necessary, and was imitated by a scraped line if not already there. The means of hollowing undercut spaces, as in bowls with incurving edges, or vases with necks, is not clearly shown. Narrow bars were slipped up the axis of a vase and then turned across it, and were twisted around by a forked stick; for this purpose they were often of hourglass shape. The forked stick, with a weight on the top to press the grinder down, became the usual hieroglyph for the word workman. There must have been a series of such grinders of increasing lengths; in some instances they are shown by the irregularities inside. . . . The undercutting in bowls is a difficulty; apparently a grinder in two pieces must have been used. The difficulty of hollowing was well managed at first . . . leaving an almost uniform thickness. Later on, the hollowing was perfunctory, until it becomes merely ceremonial or disappears altogether. An evasion of the difficulty began in the 1st dynasty, by making a vase in two halves, and this continued to be done in the XIIth dynasty."

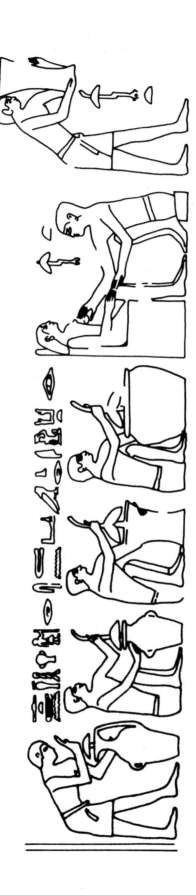

Figure 5. Stone Vase Manufacture in Ancient Egypt.

Adapted from Blackman and Apted 1953, Plate XVII. This scene is found in Tomb-Chapel A at Meir, Room A, West Wall.

It can be seen from these excerpts that there are a variety of interpretations and opinions regarding the process of alabaster vase manufacture in ancient Egypt. Some aspects of this technology can be clearly discerned; others, such as the nature of the drill bit, are a subject of some controversy. With the previous excerpts serving as the setting, we would like to provide some additional discussion of the technology of ancient stone vase making.

First of all, there are a number of tomb reliefs that depict the vase-drilling process (Morgan 1896:165; Guimet 1909; Klebs 1915:83; Montet 1925:295; Blackman 1914:Pl.1; Blackman and Apted 1953:Pl.17; Davies 1902:Pl.14; Rowe 1931:41). In these (see Figs. 3-5), the craftsmen are shown working singly, i.e., without an assistant (we suspect, on the basis of our ethnoarchaeological research reported later, that at least two individuals would have been needed for drilling tasks earlier in the process). The borer is not clearly depicted in these reliefs, although it is shown to be composed of a vertical rod-like element, curved near the top, to which is attached (at the top), two counter-weights, and at the bottom, a drill bit of some form. The pictorial evidence seen in Fig. 3,1 suggests there may have been some intermediate component, or shank, into which the drill bit was inserted. The hieroglyphic symbol depicting the vase borer (Fig. 4,2) is obviously stylized, but reveals the components which we have just noted. However, in this symbol, the drill bit is shown as a rod-like horizontal piece inserted in a cleft at the distal end of the borer.

It should be noted at this point that a preserved, intact vase-boring tool has never been found in Egypt. However, grooved stones which are apparently the counterweights noted earlier have been recovered (see Fig. 4,3; Borchardt 1907:143; Rowe 1931:41, Pl.XV,I). Experiments, like those of Hartenberg and Schmidt (1969) have indicated that the curious curved boring tool, with such weights attached, would indeed function as a vase-drilling implement. Their research indicates that the tool functioned much like a modern brace-and-bit; the intermediate component mentioned by us above, was probably a sleeve connecting the forked shank holding the drill bit with the long, curved upper section of the borer (ibid.:163). Hartenberg and Schmidt further suggest that there may have been two forms of this tool. The first was a one-piece, forked-end implement, with the drill bit driven directly. In the second hypothesized form, the drill bit was carried in a removable, but forked, shank, coupled to the long part of the tool by means of a sleeve tightened by a wedge (see their Fig. 6).

The real problem that we see in reviewing these various accounts of the vase-boring technique is the tacit assumption of many authors that the drill bit was a "crescent" (see Fig. 4,1)—a chipped flint lunate (cf. Petrie 1902:12; Firth 1930:105; Firth, Quibell and Lauer 1935:126; Lauer and Debono 1950; Hodges 1970:110-111; Caneva 1970; Piperno 1973:71). Although these flint implements are often found scattered about some Egyptian sites, especially Saqqara, they are mostly of late Paleolithic age. More importantly, use-wear observations that we have made of museum specimens and examples we were able to view in Egypt indicate absolutely no evidence of such arduous wear (cf. Hester 1976). We believe, as do Petrie (1910:79; 1917:Pl. 52), Quibell and Green (1902:17, Pl.62), Quibell (1905:Pl.63), Petrie, MacKay and Wainwright (1910:44, Pl.39,2) and Borchardt (1907:Abb.129) that lenticular conical pieces of quartzite, sandstone, diorite and limestone were used as the primary boring bit; further, it is our opinion that varying sizes of these bits, perhaps in a graded series were employed to obtain different diameters in the vessel interiors (cf. Davies 1902; Caldwell 1967:188). A number of examples have been found at Egyptian sites (cf. Borchardt 1907; Quibell and Green 1902; Adams 1974a) and we have reproduced the original illustrations of one of these in Fig. 4,c. They are notched or constricted at mid point, and this feature would have facilitated their attachment to a shank, and then to the boring tool. Adams (1974a:3a) describes the Hierakonpolis "drills" as "made from a basic circle with indentations on each side to form a grip." However, there is no clear-cut evidence on just how this was accomplished. However, Petrie (1917:95) suggests the drill bit was fashioned so that it could ". . . be slipped through a (vase) neck and then turned flat to drill a wider hole. It was rotated by a forked stick holding the contracted point." Petrie also suggests that these borers were of "sandstone, used along with sand for boring out the interior of vases" (ibid.). Similar vase-grinders or bits from Late Minoan times on Crete were fastened with wedges to the boring tool (Warren 1969:156, Fig.4,A,B).

The wear striations clearly observable on these quartzite or stone bits in published illustrations closely match the types of interior striations noted on ancient alabaster vessels in Egypt (cf. Adams 1974a:45).

However, despite our belief that the "crescents" were not the primary tool in ancient Egyptian vase drilling, we must call attention to the data reported by Caton-Thompson and Gardner (1934) from gypsum works in the Fayum depression. Theirs is a detailed study, parts of which we have reprinted in an Appendix 2. In the excavations of the workshops and related areas Umm-es-Sawan (dating to the Old Kingdom) two major types of flint tools were found and were linked to gypsum-working, including the production of vases. "Pebble hand-picks" were apparently used in extracting the gypsum. Crescentic flints, numbering close to 2000 and often caked with gypsum (Caton-Thompson and Gardner 1934:105), were classified as "drills" or "grinders". Several sub-types are present, and there were also grinders or borers of the type described in the paragraphs above. The crescents were discovered in contexts that indicate their use in gypsum-working, perhaps the drilling (or "grinding", as the authors describe it) of platters, vases and other objects. Interestingly, some of the specimens were clustered with rough-shaped pieces of gypsum, leading the authors to suggest that these represent individual vase-maker "tool bags".

This fascinating study by Caton-Thompson and Gardner represents, as far as we know, the only case in which there appears to be detailed evidence for the use of the chipped stone crescents in stone vase manufacture. However, we would like to see detailed wear pattern studies done of such crescentic specimens extant in museum collections in order to more fully ascertain their role in this technology.

Petrie (1917:44), Casson (1933:213-214) and Daumas (1962:156-157) have presented evidence for the use of tubular drills, and Petrie has published a view of an alabaster vase with a drill core still in place. Gosse (1915:45) describes such drilling tools as "circular saws." We believe the tubular drills would have been used primarily on small vessels, and could not have been used very efficiently on the large vessels such as those shown in Fig. 2.

Other tools available to the vase makers would have been copper and metal chisels (Petrie 1901:24). Petrie (1917:46) notes limestone bowls of Ptolemaic age which had been hollowed out with chisels. As our ethnoarchaeological narrative will later illustrate, contemporary alabaster workers use an iron chisel to carry out the preliminary shaping of vessel interiors, finishing the process with the boring tool. Warren (1969:169:158-165) in his description of Minoan stone vase manufacture, notes the use of chisels and the shaping of vessel preforms with a hammer or chisel. Such tools were probably also used in a similar fashion by ancient Egyptian vase makers (cf. Quibell 1935:77-78).

The fine finish which is observed on ancient alabaster vessels was probably accomplished with the use of files made of sandstone blocks, or pieces of similar abrasive stone. The reliefs in some tombs (see Fig. 5) depict the use of such smoothing implements on vessel exteriors and interiors. Petrie (1901:19), in his study of stone vessels from the cemeteries of Diosopolis Parva, notes that the vessel interiors "were ground out by blocks of sandstone or emery." A brief check of the Reisner collection in the Lowie Museum produced a sandstone block which appears to have been used as an abrader (Pl.XVIII, Illus.2). The modern vase-makers of Gourna still use such sandstone blocks for the final smoothing of the vessels.

If the reader wishes to consult additional discussions or interpretations of Egyptian stone-vase manufacture, we recommend Montet (1925:295-298), Morgan (1896:165-166), Borchardt (1907:143), Petrie (1901:19), Guimet (1909), Platt (1909), Quibell (1935:77), Caldwell (1967:188) and Harding (1971:242).

V. THE CONTEMPORARY ALABASTER INDUSTRY

It is clear from earlier discussions in this report that the manufacture of alabaster vessels has had a long history in Egypt. Periods of great emphasis on their production occurred, as in the Old Kingdom, and it seems that perhaps the craft waned in the late centuries B.C. Just when the making of alabaster objects was revived we do not know. However, we strongly suspect that it was in the early part of the 19th century when forgery of artifacts was begun in earnest in Egypt, particularly in the Thebes area where tomb-robbing and the sale of antiquities were rampant (cf. Wilson 1964:35-35,51,53-54; St. John 1852:292; Rhind 1862). Such practices continue unabated in the Gurna area of Thebes today; and since there are few tombs left to rob and a scarcity of genuine artifacts to peddle, there has been a great increase in the manufacture of fakes of various kinds (cf. Muhly 1975). Some of the forgeries are quite good, requiring much time and skill; among these are some of the fine alabaster vases produced in workshops such as the one we studied. However, much of the effort in alabaster workshops goes toward the production of small vases and bowls, ashtrays, shoddy replicas of Pharaonic busts and the like (cf. Noel-Hume 1974:298-299). A small shop adjacent to the alabaster workshop specializes in the production of limestone scarabs; these are, we might add, far superior to the glazed green scarabs, reportedly imported from Czechoslovakia, which are sold to most tourists. We observed no serious attempt to pass off these modern alabaster objects as ancient, and we suspect that most of them are purchased simply as souvenirs. In the case of the fine vases and bowls produced in the Gurna workshop which we studied, most of the items are sold to curio shops in Luxor, or are bought by passing tourists who are attracted to them as works of art.

As we pointed out at the beginning, we were much interested in the alabaster workshops of Gurna as they represented a craft utilizing a technology not much different from that of ancient times. We felt that an "ethnoarchaeological" examination of the workshop might provide some new insights into the processes of alabaster-working that were operating in ancient Egypt. We also believed, and continue to believe, that the alabaster workshops of Gurna represent a dying industry. For example, in the tourist shops in Cairo, the alabaster artifacts offered for sale have been manufactured with the use of lathes and possibly other mechanical equipment. Warren (1969:164-165) has noted a similar situation on Crete. Unlike the vessels made in Gurna, these have a "plastic" appearance. We were told that they were made in the Cairo area and in the vicinity of Beni Suef (Fig. 2). It seems to us that it will only be a matter of time until mechanization replaces handicraft at Gurna (cf. Wulff 1966:130-133).

The Setting

A string of small settlements, known collectively as Gurna, is situated on the edge of the desert (and thus on the fringe of the fertile floodplain) on the western bank of the Nile opposite Luxor (Figs. 1,2). Many of the mud-brick houses sit atop or near tombs of the New Kingdom. Nearby are a wide variety of archaeological monuments, such as the Ramesseum, Deir el Bahari, the Tombs of the Nobles, the Colossi of Memnon (cf. Heizer *et al.* 1973), the ruins of the mortuary temple of Amenhotep III and so on.

The workshops we selected for study are situated in Sheik Abd el Gurna, on a hillside overlooking the western plain of Thebes (Pl.I, Illus.1). We had briefly visited these workshops in 1971. As noted earlier, we wanted to make a record of events within the workshops, through the taking of detailed notes supplemented by still photography and 16-mm film footage. Arrangements for the study were negotiated with the head of the main workshop, Sheik Mahmoud, with the able (actually, essential) aid of Ahmed Younes, a vice-president of the Bank Misr in Cairo (Younes also served as our interpreter). The sheik agreed to let us carry out our study, and later, sold us a set of vase-making tools, vases and other artifacts relating to the workshop.[3] These are now in the Lowie Museum of Anthropology at the University of California, Berkeley.

Quarrying of the Alabaster

The alabaster used in the workshops we recorded at Sheik Abd el Gurna is reported to come from the mountains of Nag' Hammadi, on the way to Akaba. Because of military restrictions in force on Americans in Egypt in 1971 and 1972, it was impossible for us to visit this source. Our interviews at the workshop yielded the following details about the quarry and the quarrying process.

The quarrying and transport of alabaster to the Gurna workshops involves six men. Three men accompany a donkey train to and from the quarry (actually, a series of quarrying

---

[3] The purchase of this museum collection was somewhat difficult to arrange, as the sheik thought that we were aiming to set up a rival vase-making operation. "Why else," he asked, "would anyone want to buy a set of tools?" The tools purchased at the workshop are illustrated in Plates IX-XIII.

localities), while three remain at the quarry to work the stone. Once the caravan has made a round trip, the men switch tasks. According to the sheik who administered our workshop, this process goes on year-round without interruption. We did not determine whether these quarry workers supplied both Sheik Mahmoud's workshops as well as others in the area, although we suspect the latter to be the case. The distance to the quarry area is approximately 50 km, and the trip takes about 24 hours, with frequent rest stops. Each donkey in the train is loaded with either two pieces of alabaster (examples we saw were about 14 inches long and weighed 30-35 kilos) or with several (up to six) smaller chunks (Pl.I, Illus.2,3). The sheik claimed that the maximum load was 80 kilos per animal. According to the men who arrived with a donkey-train at the workshop during our study, the alabaster is quarried out in large pieces and is then trimmed for transport to Gurna. These quarry-workers spoke of many different sources of alabaster in the mountains near Nag' Hammadi, stating that once a particular source was exhausted, they simply moved on to another. According to them, there is still "much alabaster" in the region.

At the quarries, a large pry bar (over one meter in length) is used, and is hammered at one end with a large sledge; with these two basic tools, large chunks of alabaster are detached. Sometimes they use a small chisel (about 50 cm long) to chip an opening or notch in a large exposure of alabaster; then, the large pry bar is pounded in, opening a larger crack in the exposure, and eventually splitting off a suitably-sized chunk.

Once secured through quarrying, the alabaster chunks are roughly hammer-dressed, loaded on the donkeys in wide-gauge netting and transported to the workshops (Pl.I, Illus.2,3). We were unable to record the payment received for these blocks when delivered at the workshops.

The Workshops

Although the workshops we studied initially appeared to us to represent one single workshop setting, further investigation (reported below) revealed that there were actually two, one controlled by the sheik, the other by his nephew. A plan of the workshop and adjacent buildings is shown in Fig. 6.

The workshops are located in the open, with only a small portion shaded by a straw roof extending from an adjacent building (see Fig. 6). Tools, however, were stored inside a large room (Fig. 6), where they were scattered in the dust in a state of great disarray (Pl.II, Illus.2). In a small room adjacent to the tool room was a small display area, containing a table with curios and small vessels made of alabaster and limestone. The inquisitive and naive tourists are led to this room to observe some of the products of the workshops. In a small back room (Fig. 6), was a storage facility for unworked alabaster. This room was filled with chunks and roughly-shaped pieces of varying sizes.

The largest of the two workshop areas, that controlled by Sheik Mahmoud, is shown as workshop A in Fig. 6; the smaller, but immediately adjacent, workshop controlled by the sheik's nephew, is shown as workshop B. In this second workshop, there is also a small-scale scarab-making industry (mentioned above) going on inside the building shown in Fig. 6.

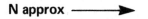

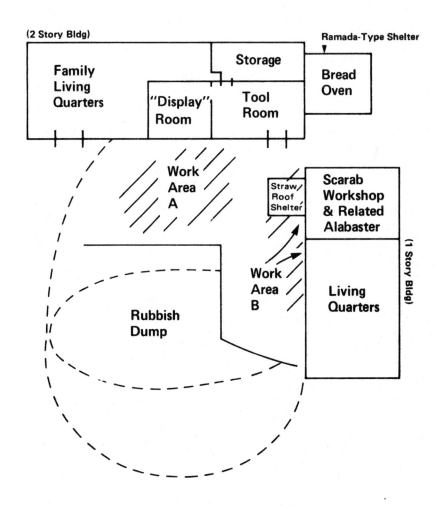

Figure 6.　Plan of the Alabaster Workshop.
Plan of work areas and associated buildings related to the workshops studied in 1972. Not to scale.

At the corner where these two workshops meet, there is a ramada-like structure in which is located a bread oven (Fig. 6). This is used by the alabaster workers during the final states of vessel production.

A widely dispersed rubbish heap is observed at the front (east side) of the two workshops (Fig. 6; Pl.III, Illus.3). Although we carried out no excavations in this mound, we checked the surface carefully and noted little in the way of broken workshop debris. In fact, we recall observing only a single small piece of a ruined vase. Some additional comments on this phenomenon are provided later.

The Manufacturing Sequence

In this section, we will describe the stages of manufacture involved in the production of alabaster vases in these workshops. We have previously noted that the alabaster arrives from the quarry in roughly-shaped blocks (Pl.IV). The worker selects a block from the storeroom and proceeds to trim it, using a short-handled double-pointed hammer (see Pl.V, Illus.1; see also Pl.IX, Illus.1). Using this tool, the block is given further shape and is reduced until the general, though still irregular, vessel outline can be seen (Pl.II, Illus.1). The vase "preform" is then prepared for the hollowing-out of the interior cavity. The most common practice we observed is as follows: melted glue is applied to the exterior of the preform and on this alabaster dust is liberally sprinkled. Strips of glue-soaked cloth are then wrapped tightly around the preform. This coating of glue, alabaster dust and cloth is then allowed to dry and harden (see Pl.VI). The workers believe that this coating helps to prevent breakage of the vessel preform during the hollowing-out process.

Once a bowl or vase has been coated in this manner, and the coating allowed to dry and harden, the forming of the interior can then begin. Initial hollowing is done with a hand-held three-pronged iron chisel (Pl.IX, Illus.2). Once a rough and fairly shallow concavity has been formed in this manner, the interior is coated with a concoction of glue and alabaster dust, which, according to the workers, "goes inside the stone and hardens it." Given the porous nature of this rather poor quality alabaster, there may be some value to this practice.

For drilling out the interior (or in some cases, for boring and smoothing the interior of a hand-chiseled concavity), a brace-and-bit tool is used. The various components of this composite tool are shown in Plates X,XI. Depending on the type of vessel to be bored, the worker will select (from the tool room) the needed drill bits, insert them into the shank, where they are held in place with short iron keys or wedges (see Pl.II, Illus.3,4, Pls.X,XI). The assembled tool is then turned in a rotary motion to enlarge the interiors of the vessel (Pls.III,IX). While turning the crank drill, the worker would occasionally reverse the motion, though it was mainly clockwise due to the fact that all of the workers were right-handed.

Before the drilling process begins, the workmen (usually two are involved; see Pl.III, Illus.1,2) locate a shallow, previously dug pit in the earth in the workshop area, scoop out the accumulated dust and dirt and set the vessel in this. For boring the interior of a deep vessel, a single broad drill bit, with serrated edges, is used (Pl.XII). To bore out the basin of a shallow bowl, three crescentic-shaped serrated bits are assembled (Pl.II, Illus.4). During the boring or drilling process, the bits may be changed, or their arrangement altered, several times.[4] For example, in boring the basin of a bowl, a worker first assembled for crescent-shaped blades and turned the brace-and-bit for a few minutes until a minor degree of smoothing had been accomplished. The accumulated alabaster dust was then poured out and the drill blades reassembled, this time removing one of the original three. After 20 additional minutes of basin-grinding, the drill component was reset with two crescent blades. But, some 20 minutes later, the three-blade arrangement was again used until the boring-grinding process was completed. On vases and other specimens the size of the drill bits will occasionally vary in order to make the inner contours of the vessel. See Plates XII and XIII for illustrations of the various types of bits. After the interior of a vessel has been bored out, the glue and cloth coating is stripped off, using the short-handled pick-hammer; this usually takes about 20-30 minutes for a large vase (cf. Pl.VI, Illus.1). At this point, attention turns to finishing the exterior of the vessel. The vessel, during manufacture, has a roughly shaped exterior which is suggestive of the final form it will have. The drilling out of the interior initially produces a thick-walled vessel with a rough exterior, though often the walls are not more than 1.5 cm thick at this point. Still, rat-tailed files are used to provide a roughly-smoothed exterior surface (Pl.VII, Illus.1), with the workman bracing the vessel with his feet and with short pegs driven into the ground. But, to provide a smooth finish, a sandstone polisher is used (Pl.VII, Illus.2,3). A large basket of sandstone chunks (which the workers told us came from the nearby ruins of Medinet Habu) is brought out, and a suitable piece (unshaped) is selected for use as a vessel polisher. The ultimate polish is given the exterior with a piece of coarse commercial sandpaper. The vessel is then placed in a bread oven in the nearby ramada and is heated for about five minutes. It is then brought back to the workshop and candle wax is applied to the surfaces, melting into the heated stone. The wax used in these two workshops is "Alexandria Wax," described by the workers as "having a good smell." The wax serves to enhance the color of the stone (turning it a light brown), and the workers believe that it "removes" any alabaster dust remaining on the specimen. The finished, waxed vessel is then polished with a piece of cloth.

Socioeconomics and Organization of the Workshop

The alabaster industry studied by us actually consisted of two workshops, side by side, claiming to be of one family, yet manifesting a rivalry of sorts between the two. Sheik Mahmoud claimed that all the alabaster workshops in the Gurna vicinity were controlled by a single family. He asserted that his father had invented the tools of the trade, a fact that we could not substantiate. At least in the two workshops that we studied, all of the workers claimed to be related. The

---

[4] Hodges (1964:104) notes, in his discussion of vase drilling, that "drill holes may have to be enlarged, as would be the case in forming the interior of a narrow-necked stone vase. This can be done by abrading with a hooked-bit of metal . . . and where the interior is excessively enlarged, progressively larger hooked bits may have to be used."

sheik had been in the alabaster workshop industry for most of his 80 years.[5] He told us that he had eight sons, four of whom were dead, with the surviving four presently employed in alabaster-working. The adjacent workshop belongs to the sheik's nephew, but retained a considerable degree of autonomy. Separate negotiations had to be conducted with the nephew in order for us to film and to talk with his workmen. The sheik told us that his brother had a workshop on the south side of Gurna, and the two other workshops in the village were also administered by family members. We did not have a chance to visit these. In the sheik's workshop were five workers (Pl.VIII) and in the adjacent nephew's, there were three. According to the sheik, his brother's workshop had four workers, and there were three and two workers respectively at the other workshops mentioned above.

The work-day at the sheik's workshop was from 7 a.m. to 12 noon. Each worker received 50 piastres to 1 LE compensation per day, plus, the Sheik claimed, 30 piastres an hour for "overtime." This appears to be their primary (if not sole) means of support. He informed us that the average income (profit?) for his workshop was about 70 LE per month. In addition to paying the worker's salaries, the sheik also provided their lunch. According to the sheik, he absorbs the financial loss if a vessel is broken during manufacture, i.e., it is not deducted from the worker's salary. We could not independently verify this assertion. However, it seemed to us that there was very little breakage during the vase-making process; during our study, no vessels were broken. We noted in the rubbish dump a single fragment of a small vase broken during the drilling process (the exterior was covered with the glue and cloth coating). We suspect that any fragments resulting from a broken vessel are usually reworked into smaller alabaster artifacts.

Based on our observations and estimates and prolonged conversations with the workshop personnel, it takes about seven days to make a vase roughly 11.5 inches high and 6.5 inches in diameter. A shallow bowl (similar to the one in Pl.XV), 12.5 inches in diameter and five inches high, takes about four days to manufacture. The vase would sell for about 5 LE, and the bowl for about the same amount. The glue which is used for coating and hardening the stone comes in sheets adhering to chicken-wire and costs about 70 piastres per kilo.

Because of the erratic nature of production at the workshop, it is hard to ascertain just how many vessels are made and sold each month. We did not observe a workman taking a vessel preform and following through with manufacture in a continuing sequence. Rather, each workman, or apparently several workmen, will work on several vases simultaneously, each vessel often at a different stage of manufacture. We would estimate perhaps as many as 100 or as few as 60 vessels are made in a month in these two workshops. In addition to making the various large and small vases and bowls (see Pls.XIV-XVIII for views of vessels made at the workshop), the workers also produce alabaster ashtrays replete with a pharaonic head on one side and an obelisk on the other, small sphinxes and other curios. These are generally

---

[5] It is hard to believe that there is no effect on the lungs of breathing the fine crystalline dust. Sheik Mahmoud denied this when we asked him, and said that in fact the alabaster powder was good for you. And as evidence, he leaned over, scooped up a handful, put it in his mouth, chewed and swallowed it.

sold to the passing tourist; on occasion, a large vessel will be sold to a tourist. However, most of the vessels apparently go to curio shops in Luxor. The dealer pays 5-6 LE for the vessel, and then marks up the price in his shop to around 18 LE. Sheik Mahmoud believed that the products of his workshop were often represented by the curio peddlers as ancient pieces.

We noted no particular specialization among the workers, each being able to handle any of the tasks required during the manufacturing process. Workers often start as young as 12 years of age (at present, the sheik's youngest worker is 17 and has been employed for 5 years). Sometimes younger children of the workers are pressed into service to aid in the polishing of the vessels. As we noted above, in the actual sequence of production, a vessel is rarely (if ever) taken from beginning to completion by one worker. We observed vessels started by one man being worked on by another and other vessels casually passed around and worked on by various craftsmen.

Sheik Mahmoud was very interested in mechanizing his workshop, as he claimed he could not meet the demand for its products. He had heard of the alabaster workshops nearer to Cairo in which lathes and other mechanized techniques are being used to turn out alabaster vessels. There seems little doubt that within a few years the mechanization of the alabaster folk-industry at Sheik Abd-el-Gurna will have been accomplished.

VI. EXAMINATION OF MUSEUM SPECIMENS

Having summarized the opinions of various Egyptologists on the methods of stone vase manufacture and having conducted a rather detailed study of a contemporary vase-making workshop, we felt it would be of interest to examine a series of ancient Egyptian alabaster vases. In light of our research, we hoped that some new insights might be forthcoming from a brief study of such specimens. A series of alabaster vessels from the Reisner collection, Lowie Museum of Anthropology (Berkeley), were selected (Pls.XIX-XXI). Most are from tomb contexts of Predynastic and Old Kingdom age.

First of all, we noted a number of poorly-made alabaster vases, with the interiors roughly hollowed out (often to a conical shape) and quite shallow; the walls of these vessels were left thick. Such vases were undoubtedly manufactured solely as mortuary offerings, "substitutes" for the alabaster vessels used in everyday life (cf. Baumgartel 1955:115). One such specimen (6-10253) is illustrated in Pl.XIX, Illus.1; it is complete and is fashioned of limestone (height: 112 mm; width: 93 mm). It has a shallow conical interior (depth: 38 mm), with bold, stepped grinding grooves on the interior walls and a pronounced pit ("dimple") at the bottom of the cavity. The exterior is hammer-dressed. What is of particular interest here is the apparent use of drill bits of different sizes in boring out the interior.

Other attributes apparently reflecting vase-making technology were observed on several other vessels, most of these more finely made and closely resembling those still being manufactured in the Gurna workshops. We have summarized our observations on these below:

6-382 (Pl. XX, Illus. 1)

This is a large, straight-sided vessel, split longitudinally. The interior walls exhibit fine circular grinding striations or grooves. There is a flat, circular depression at the bottom. The interior cavity is 250 mm deep; width at the top is 98 mm; at the bottom, 62 mm.

6-2134 (Pl. XIX, Illus. 2)

This is a small vase, split longitudinally. It has a rather shallow interior cavity (90 mm deep) and a very thick base (52 mm). Like specimen 6-10253, the interior reveals a series of stepped grooves and a circular pit at the bottom. Again, there is the indication that various-sized drill bits were inserted into the interior as boring progressed.

6-14392 (Pl. XX, Illus. 3)

This is very similar to the small flanged vessels still being made in Gurna (cf. Pls. XXII, XVIII). The interior (45 mm deep) exhibits rough, coarse grinding marks, expanding near the bottom, and with a pit or depression at the bottom. Height of the vessel is 93 mm; maximum diameter is 75 mm.

6-16429 (not illustrated)

The small vase is split longitudinally, revealing an interior cavity (73 mm deep) with rough, circular boring grooves. There is a very pronounced depression at the bottom. Height of the vessel is 86 mm; maximum diameter is 35 mm.

6-2120 (Pl. XIX, Illus. 3)

The vessel is complete. It is thick and heavy, with a semi-conical depression 88 mm deep. There are bold grinding striations on the interior walls. However, the grinding marks are skewed to one side, as if the bit had "slipped" at the beginning of the boring process, causing a widening of the vessel mouth on one side. Vessel height is 130 mm; maximum diameter is 108 mm.

6-10018 (Pl. XXI)

This is a large vase, split longitudinally. As the illustration indicates, there are fine grinding striations on the interior. Very similar kinds of vases are being made at Gurna today. Vessel height is 170 mm; maximum diameter is 108 mm.

6-10142 (Pl. XX, Illus. 2)

This small, complete vessel has fine, neatly-spaced grinding marks on the interior (depth of cavity: 90 mm) as on previously described vessels, but have a wavy character. Again, there is a pit at the bottom of the interior cavity. The vase is 102 mm high and has a maximum diameter of 47 mm.

6-10055 (not illustrated)

The specimen is fragmentary and consists of the flat base of a limestone vessel. Of interest from a technological standpoint is evidence that the bit broke through the interior concavity while drilling the base. Apparently the vasemaker was trying to thin the base of the vessel. However, the drilling process at the base of the concavity, again leaving a pit-like depression, perforated the basal wall.

There are hundreds of other alabaster vessels in the Reisner collection, and, of course, in other museums. However, our casual inspection of these and a limited number of other examples leads us to suggest the following ideas regarding the vase-boring process in these early alabaster vessels. First of all, it would appear that drill bits of differing diameters were used. The bits may have been of a variety of stone, both fine and coarse. This is indicated by broad, coarse interior grinding marks (left by coarse-grained quartzite bits?) versus fine grinding striations which would seemingly result from the use of a borer of fine-grained stone. It is likely that the coarser (and harder?) bits would have been used in the initial boring stage, while the fine-grained bits would have been used when the interior cavity was nearing completion. The ancient vase-makers occasionally made mistakes; some of the longitudinally-split specimens here appear to have broken during manufacture, and there is also the example of the perforated vase observed on one vessel (Petrie, Mackay and Wainwright 1910:44-45 offer some additional observations on alabaster vessels broken during manufacture). Perhaps such mistakes were not significant given the sample we examined, since they were destined to be placed in tombs as ritual offerings. We did observe at Gurna, however, that the contemporary alabaster craftsmen take great pains not to break or otherwise damage a vessel during manufacture, probably because their livelihood so greatly depends on careful and cautious workmanship. Much of the alabaster is quite crystalline and breaks easily. It seemed quite remarkable to us that the workers were able to drill out such thin-walled and thin-bottomed vessels with the heavy crank drill without breaking the stone. Long familiarity with the properties of the alabaster and a sense of how much pressure can be applied must be involved in their success in working such fragile material.

VII. CONCLUDING COMMENTS

We have provided here an initial description of a contemporary alabaster-working technology in a small village in Upper Egypt. We have also summarized a wide variety of data pertaining to ancient alabaster vessel manufacture in Egypt. Where the data permit, we have attempted to relate certain aspects of the contemporary technology to the ancient industry (cf. Stiles 1977:90). In the text, we have put forth certain observations or inferences derived from our ethnoarchaeological research, but we have not offered—and indeed cannot offer within the scope of the present study—any generalized "laws" of the sort called for in a recent review paper prepared by Schiffer (1978). There are several reasons for our reluctance to offer further generalizations or speculations. First of all, our study is an incomplete one. We focused in our 1972 research on the manufacturing process. We need much more first-hand information on quarrying activities. We also need more information on the social organization and economic structure within which the quarrying and manufacturing system operates. We were able to

PLATES

2

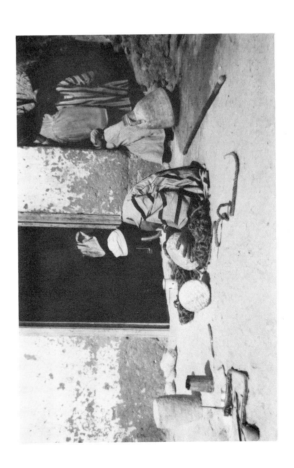

1

3

Plate I. The Alabaster Workshop at Sheik Abd el Gurna.
1. view of Sheik Abd el Gurna; 2. quarry worker returning with a load of alabaster; 3. unloading the alabaster for storage (note the net-like carrying bag used to transport the alabaster).

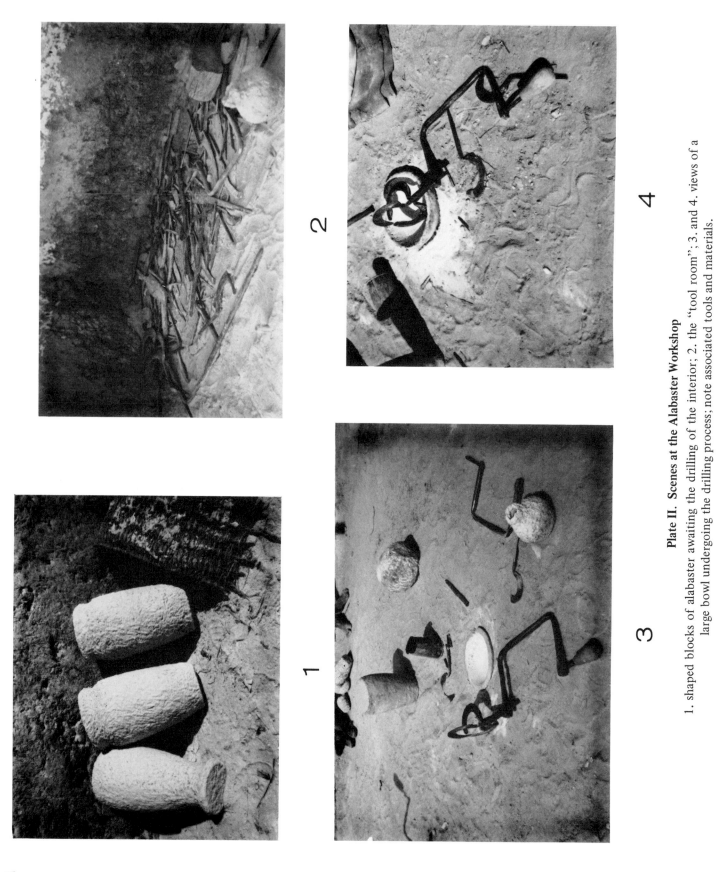

Plate II. Scenes at the Alabaster Workshop

1. shaped blocks of alabaster awaiting the drilling of the interior; 2. the "tool room"; 3. and 4. views of a large bowl undergoing the drilling process; note associated tools and materials.

2

3

1

Plate III. Scenes at the Alabaster Workshop.

1. drilling the interior of a large vase; 2. work proceeding on the interiors of a deep vase and a shallow bowl; 3. view toward the workshops; note rubbish dump in the foreground.

IV

Plate IV. Shaped Alabaster Block.
Alabaster arrives from the quarry in this form; length of specimen is 16.7 cm (Lowie Museum No. 5-11381).

1

2

Plate V. Scenes at the Alabaster Workshop.
1. Sheik Mahmoud using the double-pointed pick to shape a small alabaster block; 2. workshop activities
in progress.

2

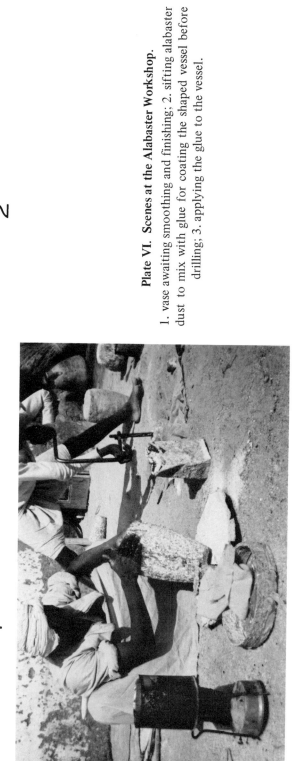

1

3

Plate VI. Scenes at the Alabaster Workshop.
1. vase awaiting smoothing and finishing; 2. sifting alabaster dust to mix with glue for coating the shaped vessel before drilling; 3. applying the glue to the vessel.

2

1

3

Plate VII. Scenes at the Alabaster Workshop.
1. using files to provide a rough finish to vessel exteriors; 2. and 3. using small pieces of sandstone to give a final smooth finish to the vessel.

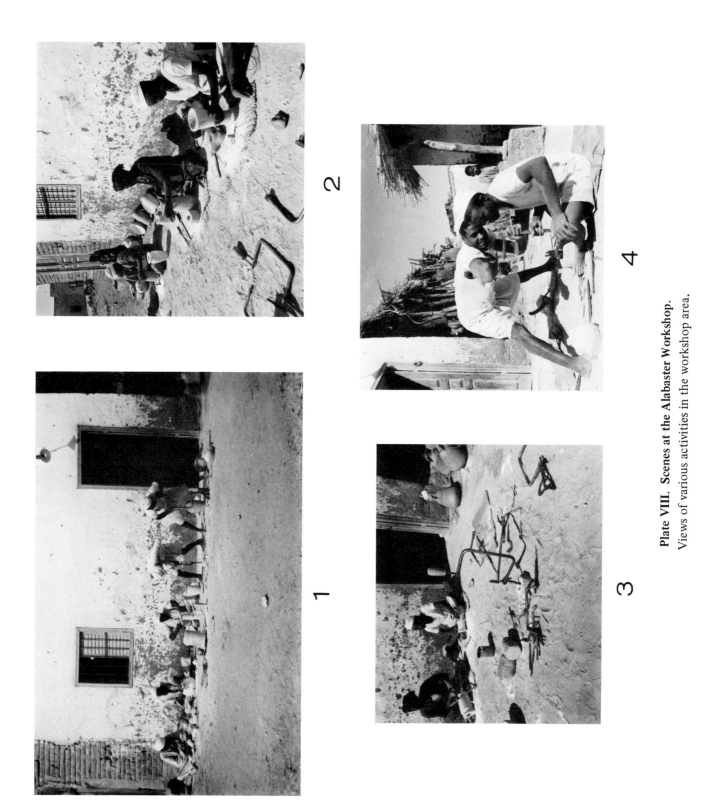

Plate VIII. Scenes at the Alabaster Workshop.
Views of various activities in the workshop area.

Plate IX. Tools from the Alabaster Workshop.
1. short-handled double-pointed hammer or pick; 2. three-pronged chisel.

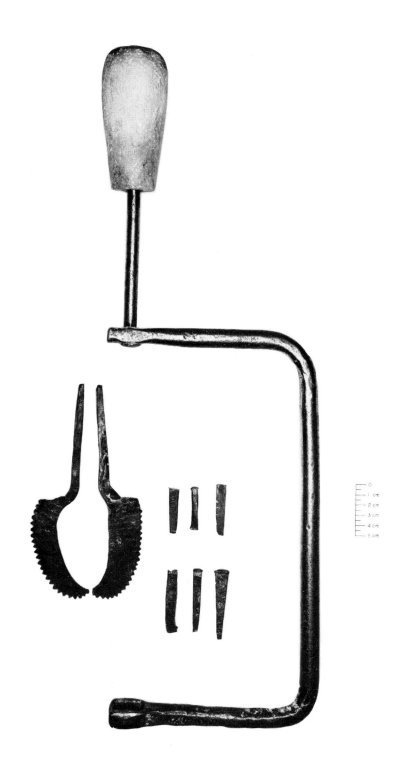

Plate X. Tools from the Alabaster Workshop.
Components of the vase-drilling tool (brace, bits, keys to hold bit in place). (Lowie Museum Nos. 5-11360A, 11360B).

Plate XI. Tools from the Alabaster Workshop.

The assembled vase-drilling tool (see components in Plate X).

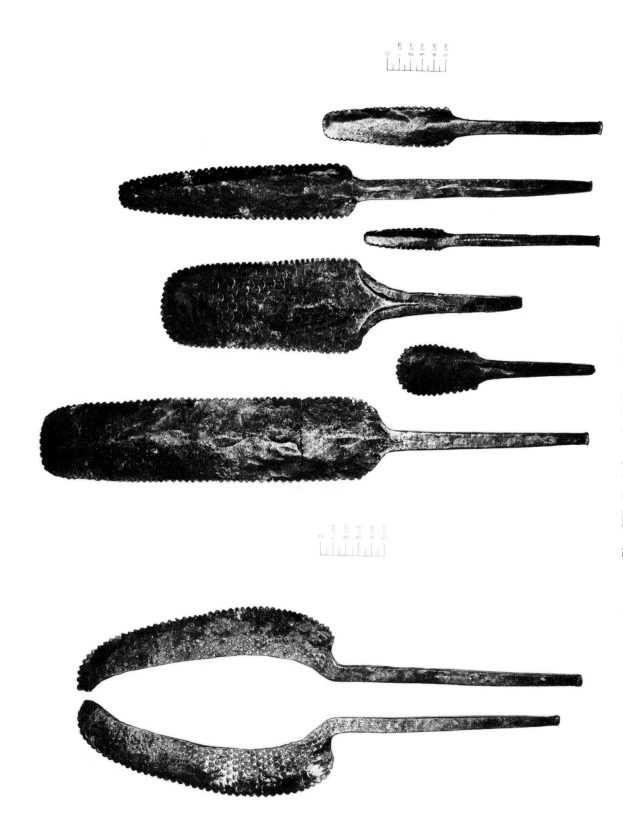

Plate XII. Tools from the Alabaster Workshop.

Illustrated here are a series of drill bits used in drilling the interiors of jars and vases. (Lowie Museum Nos., left to right: 5-11365B, 11365A, 11375, 11373, 11374, 11371, 11372).

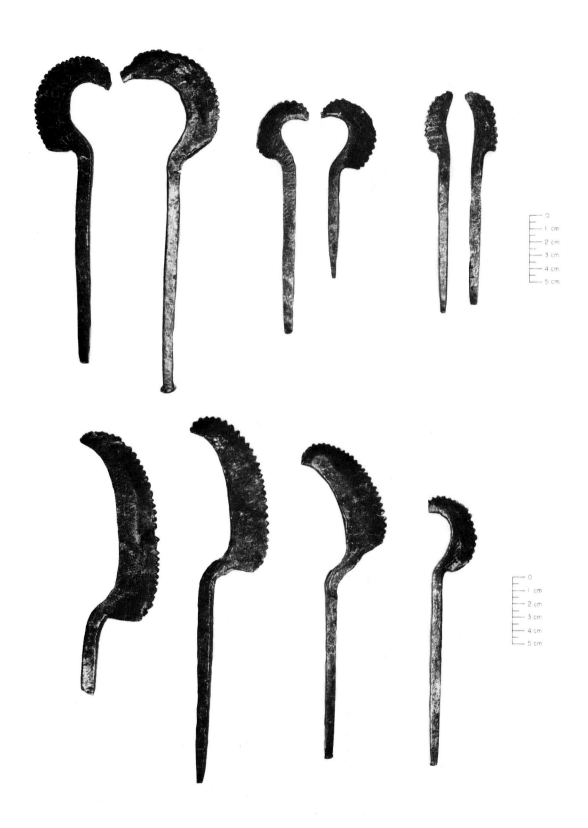

Plate XIII. Tools from the Alabaster Workshop.

Illustrated here are a series of drill bits used in drilling the interior of bowls, jars, and vases; these are used to create an expanded interior with thin vessel walls. (Lowie Museum Nos., top—left to right: 5-11366, 11362A, 11361A, 11367, 11364A, 11364B; bottom—left to right: 5-11369, 11368, 11362B, 11361B).

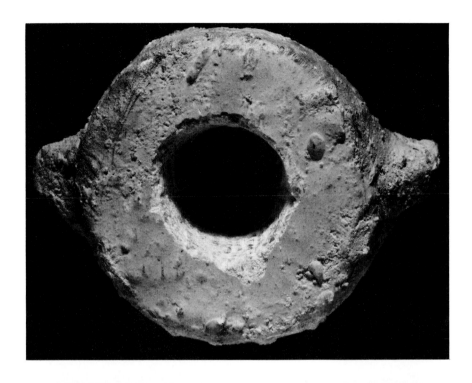

Plate XIV. Vessel from the Alabaster Workshop.

Two views of a large vessel with the exterior coated. Note drilled interior cavity at top. The next step in the sequence would have been the removal of the exterior coating. Height of specimen is 22.8 cm (Lowie Museum No. 5-11385).

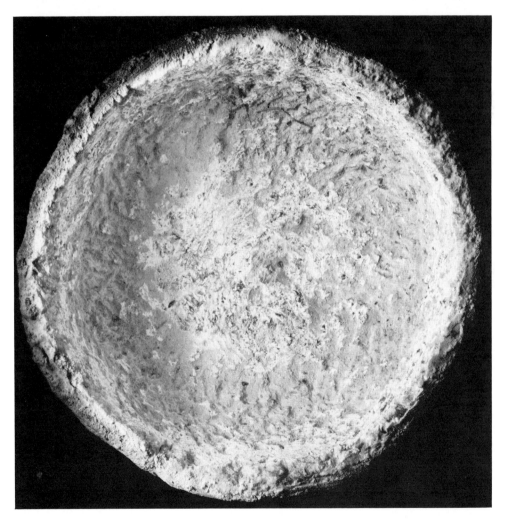

Plate XV. Vessel from the Alabaster Workshop.
Two views of a large, shallow bowl; the exterior is coated and drilling has been done to help form the interior. The next step in the process would be the removal of the exterior coating. Diameter of the bowl is 26 cm (Lowie Museum No. 5-11384).

Plate XVI.
Vessel from the Alabaster Workshop.

These two views are of a well-made large vase of the finest form produced in the workshop. The exterior has been smoothed with a file; the next step would be to give it a fine finish with a sandstone abrader. Height of specimen is 23.2 cm (Lowie Museum No. 5-11380).

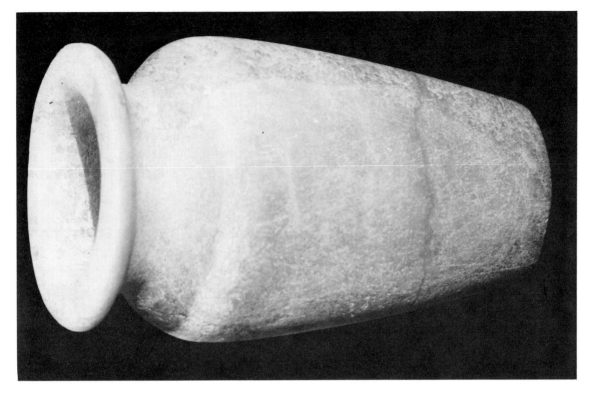

Plate XVII. Vessels from the Alabaster Workshop.

These are typical examples of the small-vase forms made at the workshop. 1. height, 13.1 cm (Lowie Museum No. 5-11382); 2. height, 12.9 cm (Lowie Museum No. 5-11386).

Plate XVIII. Vessels and Abrader from the Alabaster Workshop.
1. small bowl (diameter, 13.3 cm; Lowie Museum No. 5-11389); 2. sandstone abrader (length, 7.5 cm; Lowie Museum No. 5-11376); 3. small jar (height, 8.4 cm; Lowie Museum No. 5-11388).

Plate XIX. Ancient Egyptian Alabaster Vessels.
Old Kingdom. 1. Lowie Museum No. 6-10253; 2. Lowie Museum No. 6-2134; 3. Lowie Museum No. 6-2120. See text for discussion.

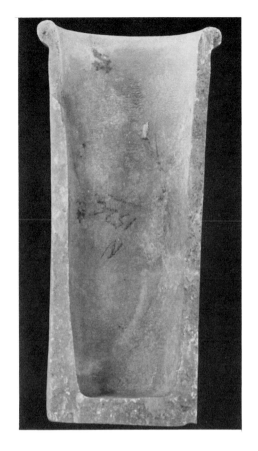

1

2

3

Plate XX.
Ancient Egyptian Alabaster Vessels.
Old Kingdom. 1. Lowie Museum No.
6-382; 2. Lowie Museum No. 6-10142;
3. Lowie Museum No. 6-14392. See text
for discussion.

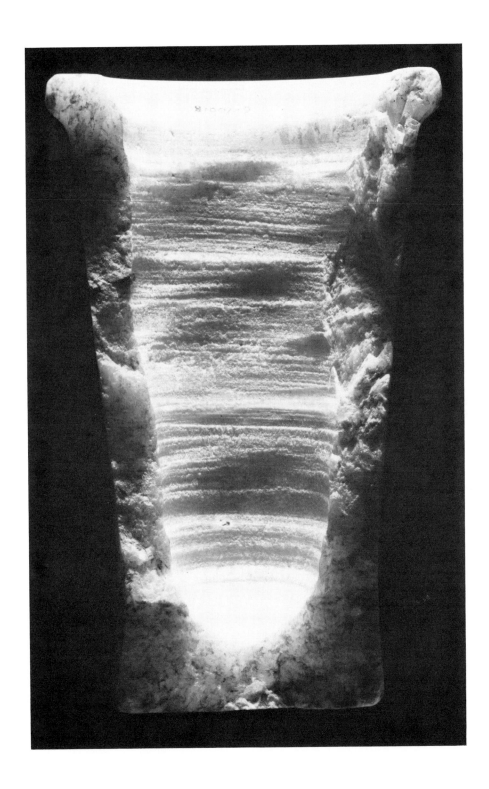

Plate XXI. Ancient Egyptian Alabaster Vessel.
Old Kingdom. Lowie Museum No. 6-10018. Note drilling striations on the
interior. See text for discussion.

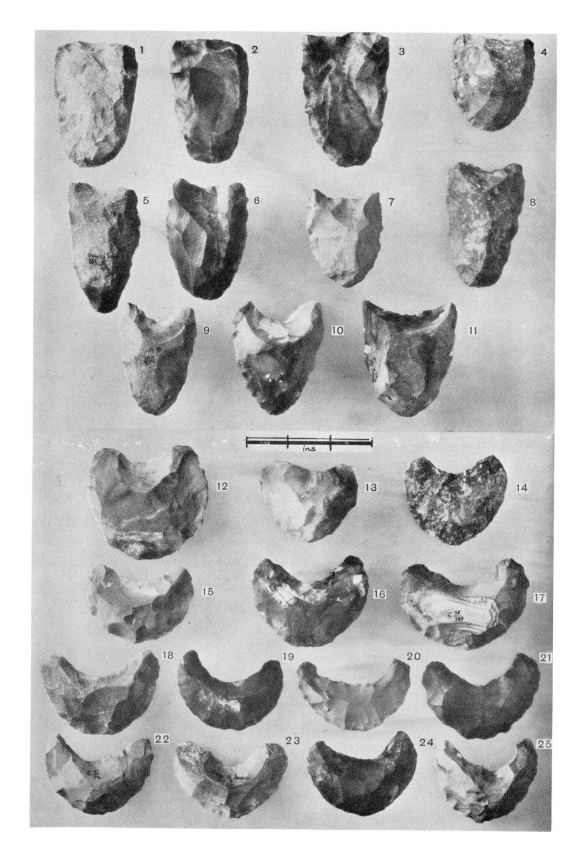

Plate XXII. Crescent Drills from the Old Kingdom Umm-es-Sawan Gypsum Quarries.
Originally published as Plate LXVIII in Caton-Thompson and Gardner (1934).

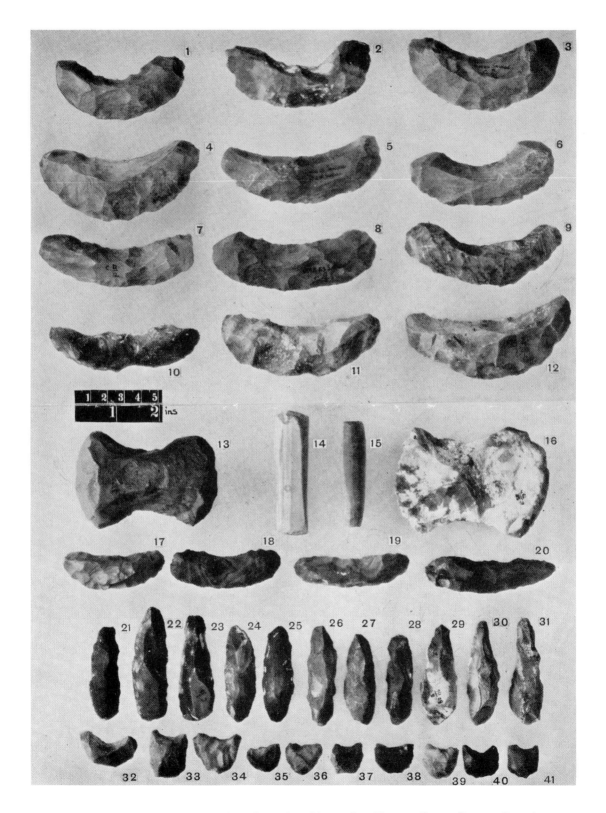

Plate XXIII. Chipped Stone Artifacts from the Old Kingdom Umm-es-Sawan Gypsum Quarries.
1. through 12. crescent drills; 13. and 16. double-ended grinders; 14. and 15. rectangular flakes; 17. through
31. punches; 32. through 41. pygmy drills. Originally published as Plate LXIX in Caton-Thompson and
Gardner (1934).

Plate XXIV. Jars, Cylinders and Discs from the Old Kingdom Umm-es-Sawan Quarries.

1. typical jars; 2. and 4. gypsum discs; 3. and 5. through 7. rough-worked cylinders. Originally published as
Plate LXXII in Caton-Thompson and Gardner (1934).

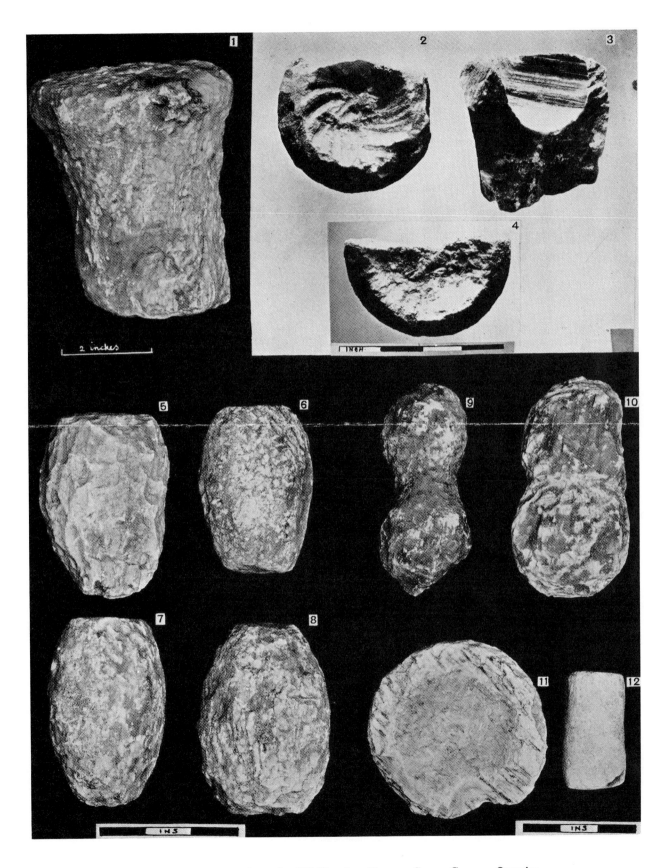

Plate XXV. Vases from the Old Kingdom Umm-es-Sawan Gypsum Quarries.

Rough-model vases: 1. cylindrical; 2. through 4. and 11. partially hollowed; 5. through 8. barrel; 9. through 10. hour glass; 12. dummy. Originally published as Plate LXXIII in Caton-Thompson and Gardner (1934).

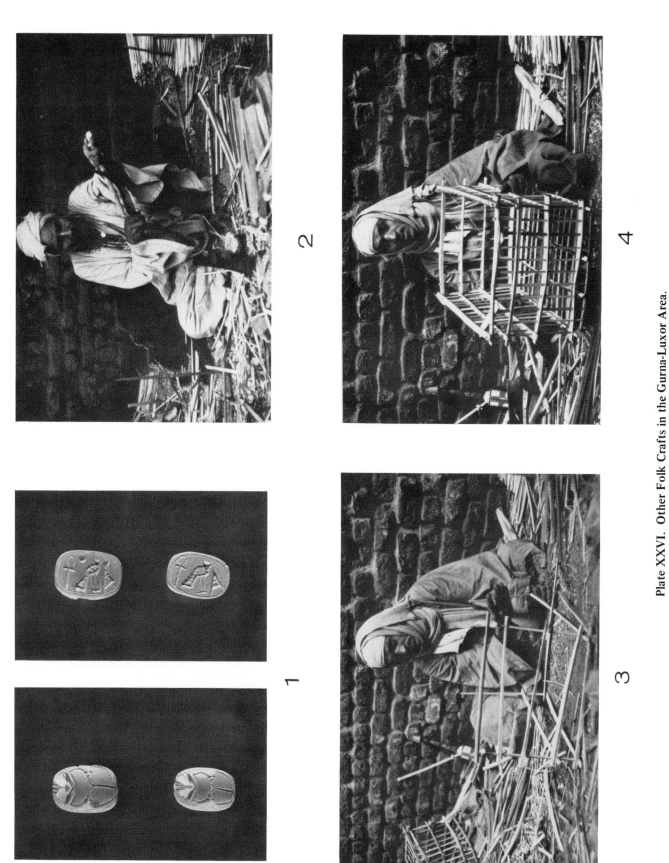

Plate XXVI. Other Folk Crafts in the Gurna-Luxor Area.
1. examples of limestone scarabs from a contemporary workshop; 2. through 4. manufacture of wooden openwork crates.

study two adjacent workshops, and did not then have the time (or since, the funding) to examine the other workshops in the vicinity. We think that such comparative studies would be essential to an understanding of the overall context within which the alabaster craft functions.

We are also aware that the contemporary industry operates under different social and economic pressures than those of dynastic times. Ancient workshops may have been more highly specialized, both in terms of organization and in production goals (e.g., mass production for funerary use, although some must have made utilitarian vessels). The contemporary workshops produce, often at a rather leisurely pace, a limited number of vessels for sale to tourists. Finally, the contemporary workshops are comparatively "recent" in origin, with the revival of alabaster-working beginning around 100 years ago as best we can tell. Arab villagers at Gurna apparently began making the vessels as the supply of ancient examples decreased, while the demand from tourists and collectors persisted. There may be, then, a gap in organized alabaster working of about 2000 years. However, we are fascinated by the persistence in Egypt and adjacent areas of certain other folk art and customs.[6] Emery (1948:17) points out that modern Nubian graves contain pots of water and food, just like the C-group Nubian graves of 1600-2270 B.C. In the Sudan, a leather shield found at the site of Qustul is identical to those still used by the Beja tribes of the area (ibid.:44), and there is persistence—over a period of 1500 years—of special forms of ivory dice markings and wooden camel saddles. Winlock (1942:193) records the persistence of basket forms from dynastic times to contemporary Nubia, and comments (ibid.:207) on what he considers to be special hairdress modes found both in Egyptian tombs and in modern Nubia (this spanning a period of some 4000 years). It may well be that while the Arab conquest of Egypt introduced new political systems, religious beliefs, etc., many basic items of material culture continued to be important in the villages and farming communities. We cannot be sure that alabaster-working has not continued since dynastic times in one form or the other; we simply do not have the evidence to support such a possibility.[7]

As we have repeatedly noted in our discussion, there are some remarkable similarities between the ancient and contemporary alabaster technologies, and the techniques of manufacture have actually changed very little. Until sophisticated excavations of ancient alabaster are done in Egypt, there will be little we can do to compare the structure and organization of our workshops with those of the past.

Our study, then, is a preliminary one. We regret the lag between fieldwork and publication but, like many other archaeologists, we have had other deadlines and other research with which to deal. In fact, we had hoped to return to the Gurna workshops for studies of other workshops, and particularly the socio-economic aspect of alabaster production, in 1973, but funding could not be obtained.

---

[6] Contemporary stone vase making is described and illustrated for Iran by Wulff (1966:130-133) and Kohl (1977:119-122). The vessels are made of chlorite, and are either carved by hand or turned on a lathe.

[7] Sandro Salvatori (personal communication) points out that alabaster vessels were being made in large numbers in the region of Sistan (Iran) during the third millennium B.C.

Colleagues who have visited the area in more recent years indicate that the workshops are still functioning (cf. the photograph in a *National Geographic* article by Hall 1977:311). In a symposium held at the Society for American Archaeology meeting in New Orleans in May, 1977, Patty Jo Watson described her studies of folk industries in the Near East, reporting a situation in which the "traditional crafts are rapidly vanishing." In that same symposium, Fredrick Matson reviewed his ethnoarchaeological research among contemporary potters in Afghanistan, noting the new economic pressures they were facing, the intrusion of new and innovative techniques in pottery-making, etc., and he observed that this is "the last decade for learning about village potters" in that region. We share these pessimistic views as regards the future of ethnoarchaeological research at Gurna, where the same kinds of external pressures are coming to bear. We hope that more intensive field studies can be done before modernization replaces hand technology in the production of alabaster vessels.

Schiffer (1978) has recently pointed out that ethnoarchaeological studies "are nowhere near . . . approaching their full potential." While we have no apologies to offer, especially since the research reported here was an offshoot of a major project in which we were both involved at the same time, we certainly feel that a more broadly conceived and detailed field study should be done while the Gurna alabaster workshops remain in their present behavioral and technological contexts. We have noted above some of the areas that still need to be explored. And, since political tensions and restrictions on travel have eased in the area, it is also to be hoped that any future research could involve visits to the alabaster quarries, excavation in the contemporary middens associated with the workshops and other aspects of this fascinating technology which were not available in the political climate of 1972.

ACKNOWLEDGMENTS

We are grateful to Professor J. Desmond Clark for his careful reading of earlier versions of this manuscript, and for alerting us to the Caton-Thompson and Gardner (1934) reference. We also wish to thank Dr. Sandro Salvatori (Venice) for his comments on this study and for sharing with us his views of alabaster technology observed at Bronze Age sites in Iran. Professor John A. Graham aided in the recording of field data.

REFERENCES CITED

Adams, B.
  1974a   *Ancient Hierakonpolis.* Aris and Phillips Ltd., Warminster, England.
  1974b   *Ancient Hierakonpolis. Supplement.* Aris and Phillips Ltd., Warminster, England.

Baumgartel, E. J.
  1955   *The Cultures of Prehistoric Egypt.* Oxford University Press, London.

Borchardt, L.
  1907   *Das Grabdenkmal des Königs Ne-User-Ré.* Leipzig.

Blackman, A. W.
  1914   The Rock Tombs of Meir, Vol. 1. The Tomb-Chapel of Ukh-Hotp's Son Senbi. *Archaeological Survey of Egypt, Memoir* 22. London.

Blackman, A. W. and M. R. Apted
  1953   The Rock Tombs of Meir, Part V. *Archaeological Survey of Egypt, Memoir* 28. London.

Caneva, I.
  1970   I Crescenti Litici del Fayum. *Origini IV*:161-203.

Caldwell, J. A.
  1967   Investigations at Tal-i Iblis. *Illinois State Museum Preliminary Reports* 9. Springfield.

Casson, S.
  1933   *The Technique of Early Greek Sculpture.* Clarendon Press, Oxford.

Caton-Thompson, G. and E. W. Gardner
  1934   *The Desert Fayum.* The Royal Anthropological Institute of Great Britain and Ireland, London.

Childe, V. G.
  1954   Rotary Motion. In: C. Singer, *et al.*, eds., *History of Technology,* Vol. I: 187-215. Oxford University Press, New York and London.

Daumas, M., Editor
  1962   *Les Origenes de la Civilisation Technique.* Vol. I. Presses Universitaires de France, Paris.

Davies, N. de G.
  1902   The Rock Tombs of Deir el Gebrâwi. Part I: Tomb of Aba and Smaller Tombs of the Southern Group. *Archaeological Survey of Egypt, Memoir* 11. London.

Donnan, C. B. and C. W. Clewlow, Jr.
    1974   *Ethnoarchaeology.* University of California, Los Angeles, Institute of Archaeology, Monograph IV.

Emery, W. B.
    1948   *Nubian Treasure.* London.
    1961   *Archaic Egypt.* Penguin Books, Baltimore.

Erman, A.
    1894   *Life in Ancient Egypt.* Macmillan and Co., London.

Firth, C. M.
    1930   A Datable Flint Tool. *Antiquity* 4:104-105.

Firth, C. M., J. E. Quibell and J-P Lauer
    1935   *The Step Pyramid.* Vol. I, Text. Imprimerie de l'Institut Français d'Archeologie Orientale, Cairo.

Gosse, A. B.
    1915   *The Civilization of the Ancient Egyptians.* T. C. and E. C. Jack, London.

Gould, R. A., Editor
    1978   *Explorations in Ethnoarchaeology.* University of New Mexico Press, Albuquerque.

Guimet, E.
    1909   Observations sur la fabrication des vases egyptiens de l'epoque prehistorique. *Société Anthropologique de Lyon, Bulletin* 28:8-10.

Hall, A. J.
    1977   Dazzling Legacy of an Ancient Quest. *National Geographic* 151(3):293-311.

Harris, J. R.
    1961   *Lexicographical Studies in Ancient Egyptian Minerals.* Deutsche Akademie der Wissenschaften zu Berlin Institut für Orientforschung, 54.

Hartenberg, R. S. and J. Schmidt, Jr.
    1969   The Egyptian Drill and the Origin of the Crank. *Technology and Culture* 10(2): 155-165.

Harding, A.
    1971   Review of: Minoan Stone Vases, by Peter Warren. *Proceedings of the Prehistoric Society* 37(1):242-243.

Heizer, R. F.
    1966   Ancient Heavy Transport, Methods and Achievements. *Science* 153:821-830.

Heizer, R. F., *et al.*
    1973   The Colossi of Memnon Revisited. *Science* 182:1219-1225.

Heizer, R. F., F. H. Stross and T. R. Hester
    1973   New Light on the Colossi of Memnon. *Southwest Museum Masterkey* 47(3):
              94-105.

Hester, T. R.
    1976   Functional Analysis of Ancient Egyptian Stone Tools: The Potential for Future
              Research. *Journal of Field Archaeology* 3(3):346-351.

Hester, T. R., R. F. Heizer and J. A. Graham
    1975   *Field Methods in Archaeology.* 6th Edition. Mayfield Publishing Company,
              Palo Alto.

Hodges, H.
    1964   *Artifacts.* John Baker, London.
    1970   *Technology in the Ancient World.* A. A. Knopf, New York.

Klebs, L.
    1915   *Die Reliefs des alten Reiches* (2980-2475 v. Chr.). *Material zur agyptischen
              Kulturgeschichte.* Abhandlungen der Heidelberger Akademie der Wissenschaften,
              Philosophisch-historische Klasse 3.

Kohl, P. L.
    1977   A Note on Chlorite Artifacts from Shari-i-Sokta. *East and West* 27(1-4):111-127.
              Rome.

Lauer, J-P and F. De Bono
    1950   Technique de Façonnage des Croissants de Silex Utilisés dan l'Enceinte de Zoser.
              Annales du Service des Antiquites de l'Egypte 50:1-18.

Lucas, A. and J. R. Harris
    1962   *Ancient Egyptian Materials and Industries.* Edward Arnold, Ltd., London.

Montet, P.
    1925   *Les Scénes de la Vie Privée dans les Tombeaux Égyptiens de l'Ancien Empire.*
              Imprimerie Alsacienne, Strasbourg.

Morgan, J. de
    1896   *Recherches sur les Origines de l'Egypte. L'Age de la Pierre et les Metaux.* Ernest
              Leroux, Paris.

Muhly, F., Jr.
    1975   The Quick and the Dead: Thieves and Tombs Along the Nile. *New York Times,*
              Sunday, December 28:1,10.

Noel-Hume, I.
   1974   *All the Best Rubbish.* Harper and Row, New York.

Petrie, W. M. F.
   1901   *Diospolis Parva. The Cemeteries of Abadiyeh and Hu, 1898-9.* Special Extra
           Publication of the Egypt Exploration Fund. London.
   1902   Abydos. Part I. 1902. *The Egypt Exploration Fund, Memoir* 22, London.
   1910   *Arts and Crafts of Ancient Egypt.* A. C. McClure and Company, Chicago.
   1917   Tools and Weapons. *British School of Archaeology in Egypt and Egyptian
           Research Account, Twenty-Second Year, 1916, Publication* 30. London.
   1937   *Stone and Metal Vases.* British School of Egyptian Archaeology, London.

Petrie, W. M. F., E. MacKay and G. Wainwright
   1910   *Meydum and Memphis (III).* British School of Archaeology in Egypt, London.

Piperno, M.
   1973   The Lithic Industry of Tepe Yahya: A Preliminary Typological Analysis. *East
           and West* 23(1-2):59-74. Rome.

Platt, A. F. R.
   1909   The Ancient Egyptian Methods of Working Hard Stones. *Proceedings, Society
           of Biblical Archaeology.* 31:172-184.

Quibell, M.
   1905   *Archaic Objects. Catalogue General des Antiquités Egyptiennes du Musée du
           Caire.* Service des Antiquités de l'Egypte. Cairo.
   1935   Stone Vessels from the Step Pyramid. *Annales du Service des Antiquités de
           l'Egypte* 35:76-80.

Quibell, J. E. and F. W. Green
   1902   Hierakonpolis, Part II. *Egyptian Research Account, Fifth Memoir.* London.

Rhind, A. H.
   1862   *Thebes: Its Tombs and Their Tenants, Ancient and Present.* London.

Rowe, A.
   1931   The Eckley B. Coxe, Jr., Expedition Excavations at Maydûm, 1929-30. *The
           Museum Journal* 22(1). University of Pennsylvania, Philadelphia.

Schiffer, M. B.
   1977   Methodological Issues in Ethnoarchaeology. In: R. A. Gould, ed., *Explorations
           in Ethnoarchaeology.* University of New Mexico Press, Albuquerque.

St. John, B.
   1852   *Village Life in Egypt with Sketches of the Saïd.* Vol. I. Chapman and
           Hall, London.

Stiles, D.
   1977   Ethnoarchaeology: A Discussion of Methods and Applications. *Man* 12:87-103.

Warren, P.
   1969   *Minoan Stone Vases.* Cambridge University Press, Cambridge.

Wilson, J. A.
   1964   *Signs and Wonders Upon Pharoah.* University of Chicago Press, Chicago.

Winlock, H. S.
   1942   *Excavations at Deir el Bahari, 1911-1931.* New York.

Wulff, H. E.
   1966   *The Traditional Crafts of Persia.* The M.I.T. Press, Cambridge, Massachusetts.

Yellen, J. E.
   1977   *Archaeological Approaches to the Present: Models for Reconstructing the Past.*
            Academic Press, New York.

APPENDIX 1

MANUFACTURE OF STONE VESSELS – ANCIENT AND MODERN*

Ali Bdel-Rahman Hassanian El-Khauli

The following notes are not intended to be a detailed study of stone-vessel manufacture in Ancient Egypt, but merely to pinpoint some of the problems and to add some personal observations and explanations.

Surprisingly little evidence survives for the manufacture of stone vessels by the Ancient Egyptians, despite the fact that, in the Old Kingdom at least, it must have been one of the commonest activities in the royal *atéliers*, particularly in and around Memphis and the royal palaces. A few tomb scenes, later in date than the Third dynasty, provide visual evidence of stone vessel manufacture, and the drill itself features as a hieroglyphic sign, beautifully drawn, and in various forms.

Many unfinished examples of stone vessels have been unearthed at a number of sites, but particularly from Saqqâra and Abydos, and these have been utilized by various scholars when deducing the method of work employed by the ancient craftsmen in the manufacture of stone vessels. The subject is complicated, and as a preliminary we must consider the probability that the technique was developed gradually, and that improvements and refinements were introduced from time to time. It is probable, too, that there were in the first instance a number of centres in which the craft was developed—perhaps in districts with easy access to a source of mineral supply, i.e., near the desert edge.

To my knowledge, until a few years ago villagers in some parts of Middle and Upper Egypt were still manufacturing mortars of limestone in a rather simple fashion, boring out the interiors of the vessels (and also the horns of animals), or manufacturing spindles from such horns using a very small chisel of iron. They spent a long time even on one stone vessel, and the finished product, it must be admitted, was hardly commensurate with the labour and trouble expended. But clearly they needed to satisfy themselves, at least, that the effort was worthwhile. Though modern—lamentably often synthetic—materials have superseded many of the traditional crafts in Egypt, the last vestige of stone-vessel manufacture may yet linger on in the remoter villages.

Of course, stone vessels are still manufactured "commercially," for the tourist trade principally, and recently I had the opportunity of visiting a workshop in Cairo where stone vessels were being turned out, using a modern technique which may shed some light on the ancient technology. Some of them simulated the ancient vessels, but it was perfectly obvious, on examination, that they were modern rather than ancient.

During a visit to Luxor I was likewise privileged to visit a modern *atélier*, which from the atmosphere and being far removed from the hustle and bustle of the great city made me think instantly that I had stepped into a pharaonic workshop. Stones of various kinds were heaped on the floor—some already having been worked in a preparatory way, while young apprentices were engaged in completing or part-finishing others. Another curious circumstance caught my eye—a great deal of cloth material, and a liquid which I at first took to be oil—were much in evidence, and were obviously used by the modern craftsmen in the making of the vessels.

---

*Reprinted from Vol. II, *Egyptian Stone Vessels, Predynastic Period to Dynasty III*, pp. 789-801, Verlag Philip von Zabern, Mainz/Rhein (1978), by permission of the Deutsches Archaeologisches Institut, Cairo. Footnotes and figure references have been deleted.

I may add that it was through the help of colleagues in Luxor that I was enabled to visit this "secret" place, for naturally the families who make the stone vessels are somewhat reluctant to disclose either the whereabouts of their workshops or the method of manufacture, for fear of interference by the authorities or the usurping of "trade" secrets by rivals. I was told that three families only in Luxor have the monopoly of this trade, which had been in the same families for very many generations.

I went round the workshop to record the method of manufacture, as follows:

1. The craftsman first selects a block of stone (usually alabaster or limestone), somewhat larger than the intended size of the finished product.

2. The stone is placed in position, and a pure liquid, a kind of glue (*ghraa*), used by carpenters for joining wood, is poured over it in quantity.

3. The block is wrapped tightly around with several layers of cloth, and in this condition is allowed to stand for at least five days.

4. After this period has elapsed, and with the cloth still in position, the craftsman begins to cut away the inside of the block, at first using a small chisel of metal to remove the first 2-3 cms. to set the drill in position; and thereafter the drill, again of metal, is used to remove the core to the required depth. Various lengths of drill are used, according to the depth of the block of stone, beginning with a short one which is replaced with longer drills as required.

5. The next step is to use curved drill-heads of different shapes, according to the required shape of the interior: whether deep, shallow, narrow, wide, etc., and again the craftsman selects his drill-heads in order of size, small to great, as required.

6. The cloth is then removed, and the surface of the vessel polished, using a file. I understand that sometimes stones and abrasives are used for the polishing, though I did not observe this myself.

7. According to the required shape of the rim and base (or foot), files of different shapes and sizes are used.

The purposes of the liquid glue is to soften very slightly the block of stone so as to render it easier to work. Another important factor is that this preliminary "softening" also hinders or prevents the block from cracking once the drill is put to work.

The cloth binding helps to retain the liquid and to prevent splitting or fracturing.

Evidently the technique has very ancient antecedents, and it is hoped to investigate in the future the possibility of this or a similar method having been used in antiquity.

To turn now to the evidence for the manufacture of stone vessels in Egypt in antiquity. Ancient Egypt, without much doubt, was the home of stone-working. No other country, before or since, has achieved such perfection in this skilled industry in its efforts to produce not only objects of utility but also of beauty. A high level of achievement in this respect was reached in the Predynastic Period and during the first three Dynasties.

Egypt, of course, was ideally provided with different kinds of stones, hard, soft, fragile or delicate. Materials not procurable locally were imported from abroad, but these were very much in the minority and were used for valuable vessels—mainly small toilet objects. No stone was too hard or intractable for the ancient craftsman.

All the evidence (from quarry and mine inscriptions) seems to show that the extraction of minerals was a royal monopoly. Although certain stones (e.g., limestone) were fairly easily extracted and were accessible on the desert edge, others could only be procured after the expenditure of great labour and at the risk of some danger. Such expeditions to mines (in the Eastern Desert and elsewhere) were highly-organized affairs, controlled and directed by great officials of State, mainly from the Treasury. Much of the inscriptional evidence is later than the Third dynasty, but there is no reason to suppose that conditions were different at an earlier period. The commissariat arrangements and military escorts were clearly important components of such expeditions.

As for the various stones themselves:

1. Alabaster (calcite) is found in a number of sites and quarries in Egypt, and is exceedingly common, as one might expect, in the stone-vase repertoire. Helwân, Sinai, the Cairo-Suez desert, El-'Amârnah, Wâdi Asyût, are the principal sources, and it is also found in various places between Minya and Asyût, and in Luxor, west of Wâdi el-Muluk.

2. Limestone is the commonest of all minerals used, and is found between Cairo and Esna, a distance of c. 500 km. It occurs in a number of varieties and colours, and of varying degrees of hardness. It is also found in quarries at Mex, west of Alexandria, in the neighbourhood of Suez, near Kôm Ombo, in Rangama, and near Silsilah.

3. Basalt is found in Abù Za'bal, near Abù Rawash, the Faiyûm, near Samalût in Upper Egypt, Aswân, Baḥria Oasis, Sinai, and in various locations in the Eastern Desert.

4. Breccia of different colours in Minia, Asyût, Thebes, Esna, and on a small scale in sites in the Eastern Desert (Wâdi Hammamât, Quena-Quseir road, Wâdi-Dîb, Gebel Dâra, Gebel Mângul, El-Urf, and Gebel Hamâta).

5. Diorite and Gabbro occur in the Eastern Desert near Aswân, north of the Quena-Quseir road, and in Wâdi Semnal (north-west of Quseir).

6. The principal granite quarries are in Aswân, the rock occurring down to Bâb Kalabshah in the south. It is also found in Sinai, in a few places in the Western Desert, in Wâdi Fawakhir, and between Quena and Quseir.

7. Serpentine is found in the Eastern Desert, in various sites such as the Baramia-Dungash area, Wâdi Shait, near Gebel Derrera, near Sikait, the Muqsim area, from Râs Benas to Cape Elba, Wâdi Umm Disi, Gebel el-Rebshi, Wâdi Sodmen.

8. Steatite occurs in Gebel el-Amr (near Aswân), ner Beir Muetih, near Aswân at Gebel Fatira, in Wâdi Gulan.

9. Obsidian was one of the materials which had to be imported from abroad. The material is found in Abyssinia, Arabia (Aden, Hadramut), Armenia, in the Mediterranean area (particularly the island of Milos), and in Asia Minor.

10. Porphyry occurs in Aswân; in the Eastern Desert, at Sanai.

11. Gypsum is found in quantity in the Faiyûm, in the area of the Red Sea, at Mariout, and between Ismailia and Suez.

12. Marble is quarried in the Eastern Desert (in Wâdi Deb near the Red Sea coast), in Gebel el-Rokham (east of Esna), in Gerân el-Ful (west of the Gîza pyramids).

13. Schist (greywacke, slate) is common in the Wâdi Hammamât and there are smaller deposits in other parts of the Eastern Desert.

14. Dolomite and Dolomitic limestone are much alike, cf. also Dolomite marble. These are found in various sites in the Eastern Desert.

15. Diabase occurs in a number of quarries in Egypt, and in small quantities in Wâdi Esh (Eastern Desert) and near Gebel Dukhan.

16. Flint is an uncommon material in vase manufacture, but cf. an example found by Reisner at Giza, dated to the Second Dynasty (Hotepsekheumui) and another at Saqqâra, also of Second Dynasty date.

17. Jasper occurs in the Eastern Desert, in the Hadrabia hills in Wâdi Abû Gerida, by the main road from Qena to Quseir, and at Armant.

18. Quartz and Crystal (Rock crystal) were quarried some 40 miles north-west of Abû Simbel, and in a number of places from the Faiyûm to Baharia Oasis.

Very common materials, such as sandstone, occur in many quarries in Egypt. "Volcanic ash", a very hard material quite often employed in the period under review, is sometimes used rather loosely in the publications. It often means "schist". Other mineralogical terms employed in the fundamental publications by excavators are somewhat harder to identify. Examination of the original vessels probably would give some of the answers, though it must be pointed out that even qualified geologists are hesitant to give identification in some cases. "Metamorphic stone", "gneiss", "geobertite", "magnesite", "syenite", etc., are instances of such terminology used in the excavation reports.

Hundreds of thousands of stone vessels have been discovered in the pyramids and tombs of Egypt. Apart from the sarcophagi they were obviously one of the most important items of funerary equipment. Doubtless they originally contained, either actually or symbolically, foodstuffs, oils, and other liquids requisite in the Afterlife. The making of stone vessels must have been, therefore, a very common industry in our period.

Many Egyptologists (e.g., von Bissing, Petrie, Quibell, Bonnet, Emery, Reisner, Balcz, Lucas, Baumgartel, Hartenberg and Schmidt) have discussed the method of manufacture of stone vessels, using the evidence of the Old Kingdom tomb-scenes and material excavated in the field (especially partially-worked stone vessels). Much of the discussion was somewhat brief.

Turning our attention to the Predynastic Period, the present writer is of the opinion that the Egyptians of this epoch, who for centuries had been familiar with the properties and use of flint, would naturally have employed this material when the idea of hollowing out vessels in other stones occurred to them. They had used flint in every-day life for knives and other objects, and the early craftsmen may have tried their hand at shaping this difficult material for vessels in the Predynastic Period, though as far as is known the earliest examples date from the Second dynasty. The craftsmen, though, must have realized that more suitable materials for vessels were obtainable with little effort, and flint was superseded.

When the ancient craftsmen needed to find a material in which the flint could be wedged so as to rotate, he naturally thought of a forked piece of wood, a common everyday sight in the settlements. The forked branch with two or three prongs was ideal for the purpose. It was a simple matter to trim the prongs in order to better secure the flint. No doubt, as a preliminary, a cut was made in the top of the vessel to give purchase to the primitive drill, and as the work progressed different-sized flints were employed. Sand, the commonest material around him, was fed into the top of the cutting by the craftsman, which he doubtless found, perhaps at first by accident, greatly facilitated the work and acted as an abrasive. No doubt these methods produced in the first instance rather rudimentary vessels, and new problems had to be overcome when more developed types were created. From the beginning of the First Dynasty the stone-vase repertoire greatly increased.

In the first instance it is probable that the Egyptians did not cut stone from the hills but collected loose stones of suitable size for vessel-making from the scree at the bottom of the cliffs. In Prehistoric times settlements were probably nearer the edges of the desert and the cliffs than they were in the historic period. In other words, the Predynastic Egyptian spent a greater part of his day in and around the hills where stones were abundant, and naturally turned to the latter when the question of 'equipment' and tools arose. It so happens that the earliest stone vessels in the Nile Valley appear to come from those areas richest in a variety of stones: from sites between Asyût in the north and Luxor in the south, particularly in the Abydene region. Of course stone vases have been excavated in other Predynastic sites, such as Merimde, Beni Salâmah, Ma'adi, and the Faiyûm, but they are far fewer in number than those from Abydos.

The development of stone vessel types must have progressed side by side with improved technology. The drill itself continued to be of wood till the end of the Old Kingdom, though the discovery of copper in the middle Predynastic Period meant that henceforth metal had a role in stone-vessel manufacture.

The drill is represented in a number of tombs at Saqqâra, Meir, Deir el-Gebrâwi, Luxor, and other places. These representations are of course exceedingly valuable, but they represent a single stage of the work on a stone vessel, as it were an 'ideal' representation, ignoring the various processes involved in the actual manufacture. These stages appear to have been:

1. The piece of stone, roughly approximating to the size of the required vessel was collected from the slopes of the foothills (in the early Predynastic Period) or cut from the quarries (in later periods).

2. The selected stone was pounded with harder stones roughly to shape the vessel: oval, tubular, cylindrical, rounded or flat. In the Dynastic period chisels and hammers were also employed for the purpose.

3. The top of the roughly-shaped vessel was cut down to give purchase to, or an emplacement for, the drill.

4. The stone had to be firmly set in a cavity in the hard floor of the workshop or wedged among some stones. No doubt the workshops, primitive or otherwise, usually had a suitable emplacement for the purpose.

5. It is possible, though it cannot be proved, that for certain stones such as breccia, alabaster and limestone, the craftsman soaked the stone in a liquid (see the modern manufacturing technique outlined above) to prevent fracturing or to make the work of cutting easier by (temporarily) softening the stone.

6. The 'bit' or grinder of the drill was of different materials, flint, diorite, granite, and a selection must have been at the disposal of every craftsman in the workshop. They were mainly crescent-shaped, and were used particularly in the making of wide, flat vessels such as bowls, dishes, and saucers, and vessels with undercut feet and bases.

7. The outer surface was polished after the interior had been completed, using a stone held in the hand and moved backwards and forwards, sand, sometimes with added water, being added as an abrasive.

8. The rim, disc or ring-bases, rope decorations, and inscriptions were then cut and worked, using small sharp pieces of flint for the purpose (particularly in the Predyanstic Period) and chisels of metal.

9. Any painted decoration was now added. This was usually in the form of wide bands, one or sometimes two, round the waist, with another round the rim. The colour was usually red, at least as regards the examples noted in the present study.

10. Handles were pierced with a long thin drill head, working from both sides.

It should be mentioned that the drill used for the cutting of the central core was tubular, the crescent-shaped heads were next employed to enlarge the working, stage by stage. The drills of various shapes illustrated on the monuments are represented as being either of wood or metal, with two stones slung or tied at the top. It appears that a single stone was employed in the New Kingdom. The drill shaft itself is of various shapes, and the workmen stood or squatted according to the nature of the work in hand, the shape of the vessel, or the hardness of the stone. Ornamental or "fancy" shapes of stone vessels appeared early in the historical period, perhaps as a result of competition from the makers of metal vessels. The stone-vessel craftsman soon showed his mastery over the material by producing vessels of floral and leaf shapes, and in the shapes of fish, animal, birds, etc.

APPENDIX 2

THE GYPSUM WORKS AT UMM-ES-SAWAN AND THE OLD KINGDOM FLINT-WORK

Gertrude Caton-Thompson and Elinor W. Gardner

This appendix contains excerpts from chapters in the volume, *The Desert Fayum*, published by the Royal Anthropological Institute of Great Britain and Ireland (London) in 1934. Parts of this report contain very useful technological descriptions of stone vase-making tools, sites and quarries. Since this volume has long been out of print and is available only in larger libraries, we have decided to reprint certain excerpts. We wish to thank Dr. Gertrude Caton-Thompson for granting her permission to reprint these materials.

The first excerpt is from pages 103-108 of Chapter XXII entitled "The Gypsum Works at Umm-Es-Sawan". Footnotes and references to original illustrations have been deleted. We have inserted references to Plates XXII-XXV (our plate designations), also derived from the volume.

— — — — — — — — — — — — — — — —

The northern rim of the Fayum depression is bordered by an alternating series of steep cliffs and intervening plateaux. As far east as Qasr-es-Sagha the base of these cliffs skirts more or less closely the palaeolithic shore-line: thereafter the scarp diverges, bends sharply northwards, and describes an irregular semi-circle enclosing a big desert bay some 12 miles deep and wide. The plain of low desert thus formed at the north-eastern corner of the depression is a featureless gravel-covered expanse, furrowed with shallow drainage lines from the high plateau, which eventually lose themselves in the depressions bordering the northern limits of the Pleistocene Lake. This plain tilts south and drops some 600 ft. in the 13 or 14 miles separating the scarp from the modern lake.

The scarp on the curve of this bay is broken in places by wadis, but one only, east of the centre, provides as ascent of easy gradient to the high desert, and this from time immemorial has borne the caravan route from Memphis to Baharia and the western desert. The northward-bound traveller ascending this pass from the Fayum depression is startled as he gains the upper plain by a sight of unexpected beauty—the Giza pyramids bathed in the irridescent light of far distance. On January 11, 1928, prospecting around the northern limits of our concession we took this route, keeping, in view of its suggestive position, a keen watch for flints or pottery. A short distance to the east of the pass, in the recessions of a small bay, a series of shallow natural shelters, caused by undercutting of the concretionary sandstone at its junction with a softer underlying bed, gave cause for investigation. Following the cliff edge towards them I picked up one of the nodular flint handpicks which, owing to the evidence at Qasr-es-Sagha could confidently be dated to the Old Kingdom. Simultaneously, Miss Gardner, skirting along a lower level found Old Kingdom sherds in quantities.

THE SITE IN GENERAL

The source from which these came was not far to seek. A small steep-sided salient, of natural origin, but enlarged by human debris, projected from the scarp-line, and stood out prominently white against the ocherous tints of its surroundings. A scramble to its top, over a mass of sherds, fossil-wood splinters, and flint implements, showed it to be composed of crushed and powdered gypsum.

Some 200 yards further east lay another, larger site, resembling a detached mound some 40 ft. high. A closer view, however, corrected that impression and proved it to be another natural bluff projecting from the scarp, its steep sides covered with gypsum debris, flints and pottery. A third similar site lay some distance beyond and was, if possible, more thickly strewn with early dynastic pottery than the other two. The flint tools lying on the surface in very large numbers were, like the sherds, exclusively of Old Kingdom forms, and consisted of two types—crescent drills and pebble hand-picks. There was an untouched sample of surface material on the workshop-mound, with a dozen or more crescent drills, fractured flint nodules and hand-picks, fragments of pots, and lumps of worked gypsum. The site was intact, and showed no sign of subsequent interference, recent or dynastic.

The thick deposits of gypsum waste and powder which covered these places indicated that exploitation of that substance had been the objective, and the source of the raw material lay, in fact, close by. . . . The out-cropping of beds were sparsely strewn with Old Kingdom debris; sherds, though relatively scarce, repeated the workshop type; crescent drills were not noted and the predominant artifacts here were the pebble hand-picks, accompanied by scarce round diorite pounders about the size of cricket balls. The relation of workshops to outcrop is . . . clear. . . .

The further discovery on the scarp edge of a village of stone hut foundations completed the main features of the place. Its detailed investigation was decided upon. . . .

We regard this unique site as a gypsum quarry of Old Kingdom age, exploited for the production of plaster or mortar on a large scale, with an attendant industry in gypsum vases.

THE FLINT TOOLS

Pebble hand-picks. These rough tools were . . . present in thousands and exact record of their number was not possible without delaying the single-handed recording work. The majority were little more than large artificially fractured cobbles which we gathered together in piles.

A remarkable sight was an area where hundreds of these pebbles had been anciently amassed. Few finished tools were found here, but cartloads of pebbles, unworked or fractured, and waste flakes, together with quantities of splintered fossil-wood, used presumably in flint knapping, but otherwise unworked. The spectacle would have been amazing even had these tons of flints been of local origins; but this seems fairly certainly not to be the case. Despite repeated journeys over tracts of surrounding high and low desert, we failed to find any gravels of comparable size; and the nearest source seems to be the great deposit of coarse Quaternary gravel on the Fayum-Nile Valley divide, such as that seen in the modern ballast sections at Er Rus. Similar gravels probably extend further north, and nearer, therefore, our site. But even so, the transport to this remote spot of tens of thousands of nodules, weighing at least 1 lb. each must in itself have constituted a collateral industry of considerable magnitude.

Away from this flint dumping ground, however, the pebble picks were also found in superabundance, not only in and on the deposits of the workshop sites, but scattered over the gypsum outcrop; the numbers were too great to be attributable to vase-making requirements alone, and their presence on the gypsum beds suggests that this was the tool used either in the extraction or pulverisation of the raw material. The heavy stone mauls usually connected with quarrying in ancient Egypt, and abundant at the mines of Wadi-es-Sheikh, were absent, and no other quarrying implements, except a few spherical diorite pounders, were found. This is surprising, as the toughness both of the gypsum itself and the clay matrix in which it is embedded was such as to defy our iron pick-axes; even the heaviest of the pebble picks seem singularly ineffectual tools for this work. Moreover, it is improbable that they were hafted, for the smooth pebble cortex, intentionally left on the butts, would forbid a bight for lashing. It seems more probable, therefore, that wooden mallets and wedges, since vanished, must primarily have been used in the gypsum quarrying to split off the matrix along its pronounced cleavage planes, and that the flint picks played a secondary part, such as trimming the gypsum blocks destined for vase-making, or perhaps mainly for smashing up the pieces intended for plaster and mortar. The tools are mostly so fractured at their points that it is evident their purpose was to batter and smash. That they were used also in the primary shaping of the gypsum vases, seems, however, certain; many well-pointed specimens were found *in situ* on the workshop mounds, some in association with vase fragments . . . the tool-marks noted on many of the vases tally with the cut of these implements.

Crescent Drills. (Pls. XXII-XXIII). The second type of tool which predominated was the crescent drill. It numbered close on two thousand specimens. Those buried in the deposits were fresh, unpatinated and frequently caked with gypsum, which still adheres to some of the figured specimens. There was a marked tendency for groups of these tools to be together. The largest group was one of fifty-four specimens, packed tightly together in the gypsum dust: it contained several sub-types, and was associated with a roughed-out gypsum platter whose tooling, however, was not due to these flints. Another group of twenty-nine grinders lay together *in situ* on the outer edge of the platform of workshop BII: this was an interesting group, for it included also splintered fossil-wood, a squared cake of grit . . . and three rough-model gypsum vases, and, without question, represented a vase-maker's tool bag. In some instances pebble hand-picks lay with them. The idea that these groups formed the 'tool-bags' of individual vase-makers received additional support from the presence of twenty spherically-shaped lumps of gypsum and a roughly pointed hand-pick, in a separate heap alongside the fifty-four grinders.

It was noticeable that, whereas pebble picks were common also on the gypsum outcrop area, the crescent drills were confined almost entirely to the workshop-mounds and their talus slopes.

Prismatic Rods. (Pl. XXIII). Twenty-two of these little punches only were found *in situ* . . .

Double-ended Grinders. (Pl. XXIII). . . . They both came from . . . workshop debris. They are narrow poor specimens of their kind; lateral edges and retouched extremities are unabraded.

Rectangular flakes. (Pl. XXIII). . . . They both came from . . . workshop debris. They are narrow poor specimens of their kind; lateral edges and retouched extremities are unabraded.

THE GYPSUM VASES

The discovery of three thousand two hundred and thirty-three specimens of unfinished gypsum vases at Umm-es-Sawan, of which two thousand three hundred and sixty-seven were complete or shaped enough to type, has made it necessary to consult past publications of Old Kingdom stone vases in order to judge the extent this material was used; some experts, indeed, had expressed the opinion that gypsum as a vase material was probably unknown. The confusion of nomenclature has made such reference difficult. In geology, alabaster and gypsum (sulphate of lime) are synonymous; amongst Egyptologists, by force of tradition, the word 'alabaster' has been given to the calcite (carbonate of lime) which was so largely used at all times in the making of vases and *objects d'art*. It is, therefore, by no means certain in which sense the word 'alabaster' has been used in publications, unless qualified by further description. Nor, in many cases, has the excavator realized that vases might be of either of the two materials. Not only chemically but practically, these two substances, the 'alabaster' of geology and the 'alabaster' of archaeology differ. Gypsum is slightly soluble and easily disintegrated in water, and has, therefore, little value as a liquid container. It can be distinguished from calcite by its relative softness, and its lack of effervescence in acid. . . . It is, however, to be deduced that a regular industry in gypsum vases existed, made either as authorized funerary dummies, or based upon the cupidity of funerary furnishers who substituted cheap, easily worked gypsum for calcite. There is no clear evidence that the vases were finished at Umm-es-Sawan (Pls.XXIV, XXV): those found suggest rather that they were there roughed out into five basic forms and finished elsewhere. Though one would not expect to find many perfect specimens in workshop rubbish, their absence amongst so great a number of rough-models is significant. Indeed in only eleven cases were there signs of even incipient hollowing of the interiors: the remainder were solid blocks only—though of remarkable symmetry—spherical, discoidal, cylindrical, and barrel-shaped. Against this view of completion elsewhere we must, however, weigh the fact that nearly two thousand crescent drills were found in the two workshops excavated; and this type of tool, specialized for rotary boring, can have been of little use here for any purpose other than vase hollowing. Its presence in such large numbers may therefore, contrary to the above suggestion, point to the extensive manufactory of finished vases on the site.

THE GYPSUM OUTCROP

Within 300 or 400 yards of the workshops in which these vase-making activities were pursued, lies partially exposed the raw material. The gypsum outcrops in a band about a quarter of a mile broad and 1 1/2 miles long. Owing to its position on the edge of a dip slope it was possible to estimate its visible thickness at about 15 ft. It outcrops in a rectangular or circular stock-work formation; and resistance to erosion, greater than that of the argillaceous matrix, has caused it to weather out in white crystalline walls against which drift sand has accumulated. The more exposed seams are brittle and pulverous with weathering. Excavation showed the gypsum to occur in vertical and horizontal bands, embedded in tough grey-green Eocene clay, in whose fissues the crystals originated. We will consider these two formations in turn.

The vertical seams consist of walls about 11 in. thick, naturally fissured in many cases into blocks about 2 ft. 6 in. long by 1 ft. deep, which almost gives them, the deceptive appearance of an artificial wall. The gypsum, freshly freed from its clay matrix, is superficially the colour of its parent bed; exposure scours off this skin, and the fibrous and crystalline structure, containing sandy and ferruginous impurities, becomes evident. The fibres lie horizontally. We freed one 'wall' from its clay matrix to a depth of 3 ft., but were compelled to desist owing to the difficulty of clearing the tough clay which could be broken only along its joints. This, however, was sufficient to expose a second, horizontal, mode of formation. At depths of 1 ft., 2 ft. and 2 ft. 6 in., beneath the surface occurred thin horizontal or tilted sheets of very pure transparent gypsum, like sheets of glass, about 1 in. or less thick, which we named the 'floor' gypsum. Fragments of this were common on the workshop sites.

Both formations were quarried by the Old Kingdom workmen. The thick 'wall' gypsum was certainly the type used in the vase industry: the thin 'floor' sheets, useless for vases, were, on circumstantial evidence to be discussed in the next section, used in mortar and plaster manufactory. Thus two industries were, we suggest, carried on side by side at Umm-es-Sawan in economy of arrangement, since neither the vertical nor horizontal veins could be quarried one without the other: the thin 'floor' variety does not yield pieces of sufficient thickness for vases, however small; nor does the massive type pulverize readily and tends to be flawed with impurities.

Owing to drift sand and scarp wash over the outcrop it was impossible to note which places in particular had been exploited: a break, however, in the gypsum seam in our trial section suggested that blocks had been anciently removed.

The following excerpts are derived from Chapter XXVII, "The Old Kingdom Flint-Work." We have reproduced those sections of this chapter, from pp. 129-131, which describe in detail certain tools used in stone vase making. The authors offer some useful comments as to how some of the tool forms might have been used, based on comparisons with hieroglyphic depictions of stone vase drilling implements.

—   —   —   —   —   —   —   —   —   —   —   —   —   —

Pebble hand-picks. At Umm-es-Sawan, Kom IV, Qasr-es-Sagha gypsum workshop. This class of rough Old Kingdom tool has not before been recorded, and when noted passed as lower Palaeolithic. A worker in the Northern Fayum cannot fail to notice the abundance of these heavy implements in certain places; the post-Neolithic lower levels of the 0. site for instance are thickly littered with them; and Qasr-es-Sagha itself is another centre. Their historic date was settled our first season. Our third season (1927-8) we were to meet them again by the cart-load at the Umm-es-Sawan quarries where they were again dated by pottery to the Old Kingdom. In appearance these implements, averaging 3 to 4 ins. in length, are of heavy nodular character, weighing about 1 lb., and all retain a rounded butt of the flint cortex; they are trimmed down to a rough point by careless free flaking and show no secondary finish; their closest European typological equivalent would be the Asturian pick. The point is frequently broken, and on the workshop sites these tools show signs of battering. The degree of patination exhibited is purely a matter of provenance: surface specimens are often a deep mahogany, whilst the flake-scars of those collected *in situ* retain the unaltered pinky-grey colour of the chert. The cortex shows the various shades of brown of the rolled crackle-skinned pebble.

A normal specimen from Umm-es-Sawan measures 4 in. in length; the butt is formed of the natural rounded pebble; the point is obtained by some half-dozen free-flaking blows from two sides leaving a blunt point and sharp lateral edges of sinuous outline. There is no secondary trimming. The implement, which was buried in the debris of the gypsum quarries, is unpatinated, and the flake-scars are of a light fawn colour. The cortex is, of course, the weathered brown of the natural pebble. A variant is formed on a nodule split, whether by accident or intention, longitudinally; consequently the butt retains the cortex on one side only. Rarely these tools are made on thick flakes....

These implements, whose numbers at the quarries of Umm-es-Sawan alone must have run into many thousands were used possibly (judged by their distribution at the quarries) in connection with the extraction of the raw gypsum from its rock matrix, but primarily for the roughing out of the gypsum vases.

Crescent drills. (Pls. XXII, XXIII). . . . at Umm-es-Sawan; Qasr-es-Sagha workshop, Kom IV. These flints, as far as existing evidence goes, appear to belong to the protodynastic and Old Kingdom periods only, and the tool cannot be traced as an inheritance from predynastic times. We have indeed to range far back to the Egyptian Mousterian period to find crescent flints again. These palaeoliths, confined mainly it would seem to the Thebaid, are, however, of totally different character and function, being made on a bisected tortoise-core, and were used in all probability as hollow scrapers; the working edge would therefore be the concave margin instead of the convex as in our dynastic specimens.

As the function of the early dynastic grinders was to hollow out soft rocks, limestones and alabasters, by rotatory attrition probably aided by sand abrasive, it is surprising that the simple tool should not apparently be predynastic in origin—the period of stone vases *par excellence*. The explanation which comes first to the mind, namely that hard rocks on which a flint tool would splinter itself away, were favoured in predynastic times, whereas soft rocks, limestones and alabasters, were preferred in the protodynastic, is seemingly invalidated as a generalization by Lucas' inquiry into the materials chosen for predynastic stone vases. Thus we learn that alabaster and limestone account for 53 per cent of known predynastic vase materials, whereas the hard rocks (basalts, diorites, porphyries, schists, granites) total only 28.5 per cent, and rocks of intermediate hardness (breccia, marble, serpentine) 18.5 per cent. Were it possible, however, to analyze results differently so that the relative percentages of hard to soft rock vases were tabulated for the different predynastic periods, we should almost certainly find that a progressive preference for softer material showed itself as civilization advanced. In any case chert drills can bore soft stone only, and it may be noted that the hard stone vase-maker's workshop at Hierakonpolis produced no tools of our type, but grinders of diorite and quartzite.

The crescent drills were first figured by Garstang in a Third Dynasty context, and Seton-Karr includes them in his publication of surface finds from the Fayum, with the comment, "'Crescent-shaped' implements of unknown use, sufficiently numerous to constitute a class. The *Cairo Catalogue* inventories thirteen...." The discovery of their purpose lies with Firth, who at Sakkara first observed the connection between the circular holes with rotatory striations drilled in waste limestone blocks, and the crescentic flint tools fairly common on that site. It was suggested that they served to prepare the building stone into blocks of suitable size for the subsequent cutting and dressing which was completed with still rare copper tools. The method would have been to drill out a series of closely-spaced holes by rotatory motion of the flint convex edge, attached by means of a wooden cleft shaft to a crank suitably weighted by flying spindles; the partitions between these borings were then cut away with metal chisels, and the block thus subdivided for final shaping and dressing. The technique sounds incredibly clumsy and out of scale with the mastermasonry of the Old Kingdom, and the theory has the weakness of not explaining why crescent drills are not found in quantities around all limestone or sandstone masonry of this period. Nevertheless, our discovery outside the Temple of Qasr-es-Sagha of a limestone block drilled by this method corroborates the Sakkara evidence to the extent of reaffirming that masonry, for whatever utlimate purpose, was bored in this manner in more centres than one. In addition to this possible function suggested by Firth, the crescentic tools were perhaps used also in the fluting of limestone pilasters and they were unquestionably used in the vasemaker's craft, and it is in this connection we principally find them in the Fayum.

The hieroglyph 'hmt,' often quoted as illustrative of this stone-grinding apparatus, does not however, portray recognizably a crescentic bit mounted in its cleft holder, but a grinding tool which seems more closely to resemble the bi-convex variety illustrated (Pl.XXIII, Illus.13,16).

These drilling tools were made from large rolled pebbles with mahogany crust of the same local provenance as those used for the associated pebble-picks. The flint varies considerably, much of it being of a banded or mottled type. The colour of the grinders in mint condition, ranges from a creamy white to dark grey, in accordance with the original pebble. Nearly all retain a patch of weathered cortex on the centre of one face.

When studied in large numbers these grinders were found to fall into several sub-types, distinguished by marked variation in the crescentic curve. The forms grade imperceptibly into one another, but the range of variation is hardly fortuitous, and cannot be accounted for as due to different degrees of usage; each shape must have had its own special use in the stone-grinding technique, and probably no series of different vase forms could be completed without a full equipment of types. In the course of excavation we come across several associated groups, containing one or more specimens of several different forms. These I have classified into:

Type 1a. **Shield-shape.** (Pl.XXII, Illus.1-4). These are straight-topped and elongated, the length being greater than the width. Possibly they are unfinished tools, still lacking the hollowing retouch.

Type 1b. **Shield-shape with slight concavity. (Pl.XXII, Illus.5-8).** The outline resembles those above except for the slight hollowing of the top edge.

Type 1c. **Shield-shape with pronounced concavity. (Pl.XXII, Illus.9-10).** The tendency towards the crescent shape here becomes emphasized, both by the deeper hollowing of the top edge, and by the greater convexity of the lateral edges.

One would have supposed the more pronounced the concavity the easier the split shaft mounting, and I am at a loss to account for the purpose of the straight-topped type.

These three variations of the elongated shield type would be of use, one may surmise, in grinding out the depths of tall cylindrical vases.

Type 2a. **Three-quarter crescents.** (Pl.XXII, Illus.12-14). Proportions of length to width are now the reverse of type 1.

Type 2b. **Half-crescents.** (Pl.XXII, Illus.15-25).

Type 2c. **Quarter crescents.** (Pl.XXIII, Illus.1-12). Of this trio of types 2b is by far the most common form and is the one figured in previous publications. The series might be of service in the grinding out of shallow vases, dishes and saucers, such for instance as these shown Pl.XXII, Illus.2,4,11. Type 2c with its wide, comparatively flat bit would be, we surmise, that used in the earliest stages of hollowing. From type 2c we are led on to a series with still flatter curves.

Type 3a. **Rods with rudimentary curve.** (Pl.XXIII, Illus.17-20). These form an intermediate group between the quarter crescents and the little straight rods, type 3b, and I am unable to decide whether the lateral edge, as in the former, or the tip, as in the latter, was the 'business' part of these tools. Possibly they are not a distinct pattern but merely the worn stumps of other types?

Type 3b. **Prismatic Rods.** (Pl.XXIII, Illus.21-31). These are straight tools, about 2-3 to 3 in. long, hitherto unrecorded. Twenty-two were found *in situ* were noted on vase-making sites as Qsar-es-Sagha. They are shaped by flaking from both lateral margins, which consequently have a sinuous outline. Some possess a blunt chisel-like edge, and resemble a small fabricator or miniature Campignean picks. The cross-section may be oval or quadrangular.

Dwarf Drills. (Pl.XXII). These little tools about 1 in. in width or less can have been of service in hollowing out the smallest size vases only. . . . It will be noted that the series follows variations in form similar to the larger series. A large number of these pygmies was found on the platform outside the temple of Qsar-es-Sagha; but only a few at the Umm-es-Sawan workshops. The largest crescent grinder noted has a span of 3-6 in., the smallest just about 0.8 in.

Y-shaped Grinders. (not illustrated). This tool which must have some special place in the stone vase-making equipment is usually made of banded sandstone. Seton-Karr figures a specimen from the Fayum, and it is included in tools from the temple site at Hierakonpolis and described as a 'tribrach flint. . . . The surface between the two upper points on both sides has been polished by use. The implement may be some sort of scraper.' I did not find any specimens *in situ* in Kom IV., and they were also absent at the quarries at Umm-es-Sawan. Around Qasr-es-Sawan, however, they were plentiful, though we collected only some half-dozen: their distribution points to an Old Kingdom date, apart from the fact that the specimen figured was found *in situ* on the temple platform with the dwarf crescent drills.

Double-ended Grinders. (Pl.XXIII). Of these only two specimens were found, both at Umm-es-Sawan. They are formed on a longitudinally split nodule and the upper face retains the patinated cortex. The lateral margins are worked into pronounced concavities, whilst the grinding extremities are convex. The under face is the more or less flat surface of a longitudinally fractured pebble: the section is therefore plano-convex.

The type is of interest for it seems more nearly to resemble the object held in the cleft shaft portrayed in the hieroglyph than the crescentic type of grinder. The *Cairo Catalogue* figures two specimens from Upper Egypt, but has not seized their purpose.

Another kind of vase grinder is represented by the rectangular cake of grit from Kom IV. It appears to have been used in the grinding of diorite and other hard igneous rocks. A second specimen is of truncated pyramidal form. A pair in basalt about 5-8 in. high, 3-2 wide, and 1-5 in. thick, lay in the Old Kingdom workshop rubbish at Qasr-es-Sagha. The under face is flat, the upper pentagonal.

APPENDIX 3

ADDITIONAL NOTES ON FOLK CRAFTS IN THE LUXOR AREA

Robert F. Heizer and Thomas R. Hester

During the course of the Colossi of Memnon research and the study reported in this present volume, we made some casual records and observations on two other folk crafts in the Luxor-Gurna area.

The first of these folk crafts is probably related to artifact forgery, or at least had its origins in such activities. This is the manufacture of scarab copies designed for sale to tourists. There is, in Gurna, a workshop for scarab-making located adjacent to the alabaster workshops. Small scarabs, generally 20 mm in length, were being carved out of soft white limestone (Pl.XXVI, Illus.1). Dozens were being made each day by three or four individuals (adult males) who seemed quite specialized in this type of manufacture. However, we should also note that alabaster scarabs are sometimes made in Sheik Mahmoud's workshop, apparently from residual pieces of alabaster or from pieces resulting from vessel breakage. The sheik told us that six or seven "small" scarabs could be carved each day, while a "big" scarab (about 70 mm long, 50 mm wide and 35 mm thick) took a whole day to carve from alabaster. He further asserted that only two "perfect" examples of the small scarabs could be fashioned in a day.

In the market area in the city of Luxor we observed and filmed the manufacture of wooden openwork crates. A narrow alley served as the manufacturing area, and three men were involved in the sequence of making these crates (used for transporting vegetables, chickens, etc.), using palmwood as the construction material. The first step in the process was the cutting of palm ribs to proper size, with the use of a long knife (similar to a machete). Next the lengths were trimmed to final shape with a curved draw knife (see Pl.XXVI, Illus.2). The lengths were then marked for perforation with the use of a palm template. A flat punch was used with the template to mark the spots on the palm lengths which were to be perforated. The actual punching of the holes was done with a hollow punch (made of rolled sheet metal), with an extruding cylindrical plug soldered at the end. This punch was 8 in. long and 3/8 in. wide at the end.

The perforated lengths of split palmwood were designed to serve as the horizontal elements in the construction of the openwork crates. The crate was formed by forcing short vertical rods of dry palm (which we did not see them make) through the punched holes until the framework was complete (see Pl.XXVI, Illus.3).

The crates were made rapidly and with great dexterity, with the man using his bare feet along with both hands to manipulate the crate (see Pl.XXVI, Illus.4). We timed the manufacture of a crate—from the splitting of palm lengths, to the punching of holes, and to final crate assembly—at approximately five minutes. Our interview with one of the crate-makers indicated that he could manufacture 10 boxes a day. He received 50 piastres for a day's work (rather than being paid for piecework, or by the crate). He told us that the normal work day was from 7:00 a.m. to 5:00 p.m., with a 2-hour lunch period. Obviously, if the time frame during which we observed a crate being manufactured was maintained all day, considerably more than 10 boxes could be made. Apparently, time is spent in other craft-related activities which we did not observe.

This brief account of our incidental observations of two folk crafts in Luxor-Gurna area will hopefully suggest the kinds of more detailed studies that could be done in the area. Other crafts could be, and should be, recorded from an ethnoarchaeological standpoint, including pottery-making (as in villages downstream from Luxor), manufacture and use of water-transporting devices (especially the sakkia and shaduf still commonly in use in the area), and the manufacture of artifact copies or forgeries of which we saw ample evidence in the Gurna area.

Forthcoming from

UNDENA PUBLICATIONS

● *A Dictionary of Nigerian Arabic*

By **Alan S. Kaye.** Forthcoming in *Bibliotheca Afroasiatica*

This work provides material on the present state of Nigerian Arabic and gives evidence of dialect change in a diachronic span of nearly 50 years; it is an essential tool for the study of Arabic dialectology and a vital new source for material on language contact and language change.

● *Studies on Byzantium, Seljuks, and Ottomans*

By **Spyros Vryonis, Jr.** Forthcoming in *Byzantina kai Metabyzantina*

This collection of articles deals with the relationships between Turks and Greeks from the eleventh century to the outbreak of the Greek Revolution in 1821, a long period punctuated by events whose consequences are relevant and still evident today.

● *Soil and Irrigation Agriculture in Antiquity*

By **Thorkild Jacobsen.** Forthcoming in *Bibliotheca Mesopotamica*.

A report on the essential results of the archaeological investigation in the Diyala River Basin in 1957-58. This project was planned along the lines of a single major problem, salinization, and approached from many directions including soil sciences, paleobotany, ethnography, archaeology and epigraphy.

● *Essays in Islamic Art and Architecture*

Edited by **Abbas Daneshvari.** Forthcoming in *Islamic Art and Architecture*.

This volume in honor of Katharina Otto-Dorn includes contributions by D. Duda, M. Oluş Arik, Guitty Azarpay, Eva Baer, Walter B. Denny, G. Fehérvári, M. Skohoohy, Lisa Golombek, Ernst J. Grube, Robert Hillenbrand, Raymond Lifchez, Zeynep Çelik, Ingeborg Luschey-Schmeisser and Gönül Öney.

● *Explaining Trade in Western Asia*

By **Norman Yoffee.** Forthcoming in *Monographs on the Ancient Near East*.

A comparative examination of *Trade in the Ancient Near East* (J. D. Hawkins, ed.) and *Ancient Civilizations and Trade* (J. A. Sabloff and C. Lamberg-Karlovsky, eds.) provides an opportunity to juxtapose bodies of data and theory in the interpretation of Mesopotamian economic systems. Among the sections of the essay are reviews of Mesopotamian trade in the third millennium and Old Assyrian periods and a concluding evaluation on the prospects for explaining trade in Ancient Western Asia.

● *Making Stone Vases: Ethnoarchaeological Studies at an Alabaster Workshop in Upper Egypt*

By **Thomas R. Hester** and **Robert F. Heizer.** Forthcoming in *Occasional Papers on the Near East*.

This monograph, based on field work in Egypt in 1972, provides a description of alabaster vase-making at a contemporary workshop in the village of Sheik Abd el Gurna, western Thebes. The study documents the technology employed in this local folk craft and relates the techniques to stone vase-making in ancient Egypt.

● *The Photographic Heritage of the Middle East (1849-1893)*

By **Paul Chevedden.** Forthcoming in *Occasional Papers on the Near East*.

A catalog of photographs from an exhibition of the extensive collection of UCLA's Research Library. The works of F. Frith, W. Hammerschmidt and F. Bedford, among others, are featured. Also included is a history of photography in the Middle East and sections on the work of each photographer.

For more information, please write: UNDENA PUBLICATIONS, P. O. Box 97, Malibu, CA 90265, U.S.A.

Cities of the Delta, Part I: Naukratis
Preliminary Report on the 1977-78 and 1980 Seasons

By William D. E. Coulson and Albert Leonard, Jr.

Malibu: Undena Publications, Febrary 1982
LC 81-52798; ISBN 0-89003-081-2/cloth, 0-89003-080-4/paper
Pp. xiv-108 including 46 figures, 10 plates; $20.50/cloth, $15.00/paper

The Naukratis Project concerns work in the Western Nile Delta, in an area bounded by El-Barnugi in the north and Kom el-Hisn in the south. This area contains the ancient city of Naukratis (Kom Ge'if) which, according to Herodotus, was the first and only city in which the early Greek merchants were allowed to settle, as well as other sites which reported histories of occupation from Pharaonic through late Roman times. Unfortunately, little is known of these sites and their state of preservation. The Naukratis project, therefore, involves: 1) a program of excavation at Naukratis based on modern archaeological methods and techniques and backed by an interdisciplinary support staff. The primary objectives will the the establishment of a stratigraphic sequence against which the results of earlier excavations at the site can be evaluated and the creation of a typology for the ceramic material. 2) A survey of all ancient sites in the environs of Naukratis in order to assess the character of the visible remains, the state of site preservations, and the extent of modern encroachment.

Issued under the auspices of ARCE — The American Research Center in Egypt

O. W. Muscarella, *Unexcavated Objects and Ancient Near Eastern Art*. 19 pp. *Occasional Papers*, Vol. 1, Issue 1 (October 1979)

The recognition by archaeologists and art historians that forgeries of ancient Near Eastern art are extensive, that they have been uncritically accepted into the repertory of ancient artifacts, and that this anomaly has resulted from a failure to distinguish excavated from unexcavated material, has only recently been perceived. It is suggested that the forgery problem can be resolved only by frank and open discussion with regard to both the objects that scholars believe should be indicted and the various reasons for its flourishing existence.

The present paper continues the discussion initiated in "Unexcavated Objects and Ancient Near Eastern Art," published in *Mountains and Lowlands, Bibl. Mesopotamica* VII, ed. L. Levine and T. C. Young, Jr. (Undena 1977), pp. 153-207. Its main purpose is to make adjustments and additions to the original publication. Additional citations and references of forgeries or suspicions are cited, more bibliographical references are presented, and additional objects are considered. There is also a brief review of excavated material from Luristan.